JOAN HAMBURG

GERRY FRANK

OUR LITTLE BLACK BOOK OF
SHOPPING
SECRETS

The very best shopping hints from the two
seasoned shoppers who know New York best,
with editorial director Michael Kaminer.

Extra special secrets are marked
"Joan and Gerry's Best Buy".

For additional copies (quantity prices available),
please write or call:

JOAN AND GERRY
P.O. BOX 2225
SALEM, OREGON 97308
(503/585-8411)
FAX: 503/585-1076

Joan and Gerry
Our Little Black Book of Shopping Secrets

Copyright 1993 by Joan Hamburg and Gerry Frank

All rights reserved. No part of this book may be reproduced in any form or by an electronic or mechanical means, including information storage and retrieval systems, without permission in writing from the authors, except by a reviewer who may quote brief passages in a review.

Printed in the United States of America.

Library of Congress Catalog Card No: 90-85759

ISBN: 1-879333-02-3

First Edition 1991
Second Edition 1993

INTRODUCTION

When we met as professional journalists and best-selling authors many years ago, we discovered that both of us (one from Salem, Oregon, one from Long Island, New York) were still having a love affair with New York City. Whenever either of us had free time, we loved to explore the city's resources and unravel its surprises. We were exhilirated by shopping in what is, without question, the shopping capital of the world. For us, shopping is a hobby, a sport, an adventure, and ultimately, an occupation.

Shopping in Manhattan is an intense experience. Every section of this town is filled with stores competing with one another to attract eager shoppers. It's hard to resist the "buy me" appeal. After all, whatever you want is here: The perfect suit for your high school reunion, the gown for a wedding, a tuxedo for the prom, a communion dress, antiques, housewares, and more. With such abundance, the challenge is finding the best sources for the best buys.

Over the years, the two of us have shared our secret sources only with each other. Now we have decided to join forces, opening our personal address and phone books to reveal hundreds of hand-picked choices for the very best shopping that New York offers. Each one of the shops and outlets was chosen for its quality, value, selection and uniqueness of merchandise. Know, too, that this is a wonderful time to shop department stores throughout the area. To stay competitive, the major stores like Saks, Bloomingdales, Lord & Taylor, A & S, Barneys, Henri Bendel, Macy's and Bergdorf Goodman now have superb sales all year long. Check the local newspapers and ask the sales help in the stores.

Before you start, keep the following tips in mind:

1. Do your homework. Comparison shop and know the general price of merchandise.

2. Know what you need before you start shopping. DO NOT buy an item because it is cheap. If you don't need it, it is not a bargain.

3. Try on clothing items before you leave the store.

4. Be sure to check return policy and always save receipts, particularly during the holiday season.

5. Manhattan streets are filled with street vendors selling "famous name" watches, shirts, sweaters and more. Most of these items are counterfeit and if there is a problem you'll be hard pressed to find someone who will repair, exchange or refund.

6. The fashion business has changed so much that nobody really knows how to define "wholesale" anymore. For you, that means

an abundance of sample and showroom sales from designers who almost never used to open their doors. Go to the garment center, or fashion center as it is known, from Broadway and 7th Avenue on 34th Street to about 40th Street. Your best bet is to scout here on a Saturday from 10 a.m.-2 p.m. Always ask the elevator starter who is open, and bring cash. Many designers also rent basement spaces now to sell off seasonal overstocks and returns; certain times of year, you'll get notices of these handed to you. And, of course, if there's a designer you love, call the showroom and ask to get on their mailing list for upcoming sales.

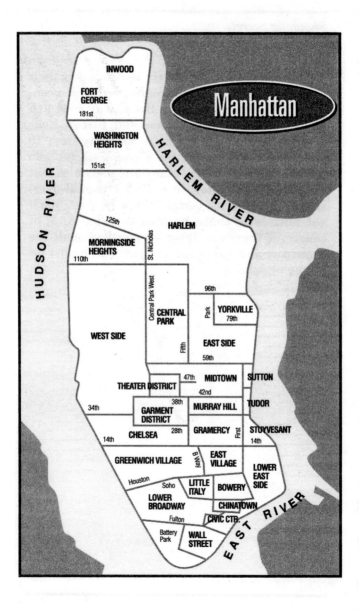

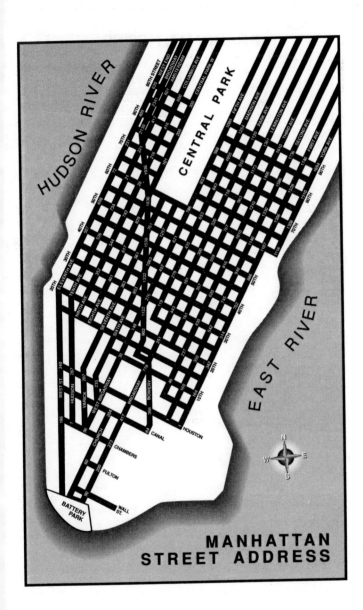

MANHATTAN
STREET ADDRESS

PERSONAL NOTES

ANTIQUES

THE ANNEX ANTIQUES FAIR AND FLEA MARKET
6th Ave. and 26th St.
212-243-5343
Sat., Sun. year round; $1 admission

Joan & Gerry's Best Buy

Expert scavengers consider this the city's best flea market; come early for finds on collectibles, estate jewelry, furniture, even militaria. Bargaining's the rule.

If it's raining, look across the street. A new indoor market's sprung up, and it's filled with treasures.

ANTIQUES AT DALES
683 Coney Island Ave.
Kensington, Brooklyn, take "D" to
Courtelyou Road
718-941-7059
7 days
no c.c.

Idiosyncratic antique furniture for much less than most Manhattan shops; we've heard stories of very valuable finds from here.

A REPEAT PERFORMANCE
156 First Ave. (10th St)
212/529-0832
7 days

Cluttered little antique emporium specializes in whimsical lampshades; you'll also find period cigarette cases and lighters, furniture, and charming vintage musical instruments.

BRIMFIELD OUTDOOR ANTIQUE SHOWS
Route 20
Brimfield, Mass 01010
413-283-6149
Second week of May, July and September.
Call for specific dates.

Joan & Gerry's Best Buy

Join a cast of thousands fighting with dealers for fabulous deals; it's worth a car, bus, or train ride for rarities you might not find in the city.

BURLINGTON ANTIQUE TOYS
1082 Madison Ave. (at 82nd St)
212/861-9708
Mon.-Sat. 10-6 and by appointment; (closed Sat. in summer)

Browsers, take note: You'll lose yourself among the charming toy cars, airplanes, boats, soldiers, and tin toys here.

DARROW'S FUN ANTIQUES
309 E. 61st St.
212-838-0730
Mon.-Sat.;Sun. by appointment

Toys 'R Us for connoisseurs, from Mickey Mouse watches to toy soldiers to '50s kitsch. There's also a trove of animation art — the hottest new collectible — from $10 to $4,000. Darrow's rents props and antiques, too; ask for Gary or George.

HOWARD KAPLAN ANTIQUES
827 Broadway
212-674-1000
Mon.-Fri.

Gorgeous French and British imported furniture, with a whole floor of oversized antique beds; bring your bankbook.

HYDE PARK ANTIQUES
836 Broadway
212-477-0033
Mon.-Sat.; closed Sat. in the summer

William and Mary and Regency aren't New England colleges, but old English furniture periods; you'll find a huge inventory of both here, along with antique accents and accessories.

JAMES II GALLERY
15 E. 57th St.
212-355-7040
Mon.-Sat.

Victorian antiques that would do the Queen herself proud; each piece of silver, glass, pottery, furniture, and jewelry comes with a fascinating little history card.

SECONDHAND ROSE
270 Lafayette St.
212-431-7673
Mon.-Fri.; weekends by appointment
accepts American Express

Joan & Gerry's Best Buy

Along with vintage furniture and knick-knacks, you'll find nearly 50,000 original rolls of wallpaper from the `20s-`50s here.

T&K FRENCH ANTIQUES
120 Wooster St.
212-219-2472
Mon.-Sat.

Fabulous French country furniture from 17th-19th century, along with antique bathroom accessories; they also import charming traditional bistro chairs.

WAVES
32 E. 13th St.
212-989-9284
Tues.-Sat.

"Waves" here means radios, and this place has a fabulous collection of vintage models, along with old record players, victrolas, and Edison cylinders.

URBAN ARCHAEOLOGY
285 Lafayette St.
212-431-6969
Mon.-Sat.

Collectors will think they've gone to heaven in this mammoth showroom; antiques, reproduction lighting and bathroom fixtures, tubs, sinks, and plumbing.

APPLIANCES

ABC TRADING COMPANY
31 Canal St.   212-228-5080
Sun.-Fri.

Refrigerators, washing machines, VCRs, televisions, camcorders discounted up to 60% off retail; they also specialize in 220-volt appliances for use overseas.

ELECTRICAL APPLIANCES RENTAL & SALES COMPANY
40 W. 29th St., 2nd floor
212-686-8884
Mon.-Fri.
No c.c.

If it plugs in, these people rent or sell it; fans, heaters, refrigerators, TVs, VCRs, toasters, vacuums, dehumidifiers from major manufacturers.

GORDON'S APPLIANCE OUTLET
Rt. 24/Main St. (Bottle Hill Shopping Center)
Madison, N.J. 07490
201-377-5000
7 days

Joan & Gerry's Best Buy

Along with discounted air conditioners, TVs, and stereo equipment, this place carries scratched or

*dented appliances for up to 25% less than other
discounters — not perfect-looking, but fully guar-
anteed to work. Take a look at their discount jewelry and watches, too.*

KEREKES BAKERY
AND RESTAURANT EQUIPMENT
7107 13th Ave.
Brooklyn, NY 11228
718-232-7044
Mon.-Fri.

Joan & Gerry's Best Buy

*If you just can't live without a pizza oven at home,
call them; you'll also find higher-end professional
equipment.*

PENINSULA BUYING
212-838-1010

*Always check prices here before you buy retail;
you'll get fantastic deals on appliances — and now
kitchen cabinets, too.*

PRICE WATCHERS
718-470-1620, 516-222-9100
Mon.-Fri.

Joan & Gerry's Best Buy

*Discounts on TVs, video equipment, and large
appliances. Phone orders only; payment by COD,
cash, money order, or certified check. Call with a
model number and they'll beat your best price.*

ART SUPPLIES

CHARRETTE
215 Lexington Ave.
212-645-5555
7 days

Joan & Gerry's Best Buy

With over 20,000 items in stock, Charrette likely carries any art, drafting, or architectural supplies on your list. Discounts of up to 70% on all major brands.

PEARL PAINT COMPANY
308 Canal St.
212-431-7932
7 days

Joan & Gerry's Best Buy

On ten bustling floors, Pearl carries the city's largest selection of art, graphic, craft, and stationary supplies — even printmaking and bookbinding material.

UTRECHT ART AND DRAFTING SUPPLIES
111 Fourth Ave.
212-777-5353
Mon.-Sat.

At prices up to 40% off list, you'll find a huge selection of tools, paper, writing utensils, paints, easels; smart sales staff.

AUCTIONS

SOTHEBY'S
1334 York Ave.
Arcade auction phone 212-606-7000

Only Old Masters for seven figures? Take another look. At some auctions, Sotheby's becomes a source for tremendous deals on antiques and rarities. Recent finds: An exotic horn desk for under $1,000, antique carpet for $500.

WILLIAM DOYLE GALLERIES
175 E. 87th St.
Tag sale phone 212-410-9285
Tag sale hours Mon.-Fri. 8:30-5;Sat 10-5
C.C. accepted only at Tag Sale

Look, but don't touch, at Doyle's glamourous estate and jewelry auctions; then visit the tag sale next to the main gallery, where you'll find the real buys. Whatever doesn't sell at auction winds up there, at less glamourous prices.

GUERNSEY'S
108 E. 73rd St.
212-794-2280
Mon.-Fri.
No c.c.

Joan & Gerry's Best Buy
This high-class auction house sells collectible ephemera like carnival memorabilia and old signs; call for auction dates and times.

GENERAL POST OFFICE
MONTHLY AUCTIONS
380 W. 33rd St.
212-330-2933

Joan & Gerry's Best Buy

Ever wonder what happens to lost packages? Some — containing everything from jewelry to toys — end up as big bargains on the auction block here.

POLICE DEPARTMENT
PUBLIC AUCTIONS
One Police Plaza
212-406-1369

Joan & Gerry's Best Buy

You'll find terrific buys here on cars, cameras, televisions, and more unclaimed or stolen goods. At least you know your money's going to a good cause.

US CUSTOMS AUCTIONS
Public auction line for information
on auctions around the country
703-351-7887
8-5

Joan & Gerry's Best Buy

Some travelers mistakenly consider every purchase "duty free;" their goods usually end up here. Eye-popping merchandise can include anything from planes to cars to jewelry to coffee beans.

AUTOGRAPHS

JAMES LOWE AUTOGRAPHS
30 E. 60th St.
212-759-0775
Mon.-Fri.;Sat. by appointment
No c.c.

*The writing's on the wall; few collectibles dealers
can match James Lowe's catalog of celebrated sig-
natures, from autographed photos of Buffalo Bill
to part of a Puccini opera score.*

ANNA SOSENKO
25 Central Park West
212-247-4816
Mon.-Fri. by appointment
No c.c.

*Make an appointment, if only to meet Ms. Sosenko
and view her dazzling autograph collection; leg-
ends from Chaplin to Porter to Berlin come alive
here.*

BEVERAGES
B&E
511 W. 23rd St.
212-243-6812
Mon.-Sat.
No c.c.

Joan & Gerry's Best Buy
*On an industrial West Side block, you'll find dis-
counts of up to 50% of regular retail for soda and
beer. If you're planning to entertain, it's worth the
trek.*

CROSSROADS WINE & LIQUOR STORE
55 W. 14th St.
212-924-3060
Mon.-Sat.

Pay no attention to the seedy block that houses this generic-looking shop; inside, you'll find a very impressive selection of wines much cheaper than uptown, and a smart staff to guide you through it.

FAIRFAX LIQUOR
211 E. 66th St.
212-734-6871
Mon.-Sat.

Despite star-studded customers like David Rockefeller and Richard Nixon, this Upper East Side supplier claims a markup of only 12%, the legal minimum; superb selection and service.

THREE KINGS
371 Broadway
212-966-3075
Mon.-Sat.
no c.c.

Financial District wholesaler offers some of the best prices we've seen on beer & soda, with no minimum purchase. Recent bargains: 12-packs of Heineken, Beck's, and Amstel Light beer nearly

*half off retail at $9.99; 2-liter bottles of soda,
$7.89 a case. If you're entertaining, a stop here is
a must.*

WAREHOUSE WINES & SPIRITS
735 Broadway
212-982-7770
Mon.-Sat.

*You'll find better values here on premium liquors
and wines than at other neighborhood stores.*

BICYCLES

GENE'S DISCOUNTED BICYCLES
242 E. 79th St.
212-288-0739
7 days

Joan & Gerry's Best Buy

*For deals like these, you usually have to buy
generic. But Gene's meets or beats prices on
brands like Klein, Specialized, and Fuji racing,
mountain, and touring bikes.*

STUYVESANT BICYCLE
349 W. 14th St.
212-254-5200
7 days

*Command central for NYC biking enthusiasts;
staff seems more concerned with selling the right
bike than just selling. One of the East Coast's
most respected bikestores.*

BIRDS
BIRD JUNGLE
401 Bleecker St.
212-242-1757
7 days

Feels more like a tropical paradise than a West Village storefront; birds familiar, exotic, and mostly expensive, from Amazons to Zebra Finches.

BOOKS
BOOKS—Children's

BARNES & NOBLE JR.
128 Fifth Ave.	212-633-3500
120 E. 86th St.	212-427-0686

Sales Annex at
Fifth Ave. & 18th St.
7 days

Many fans of this discount-book chain don't know about its children's emporium; little readers will find the same low prices and huge selection as the grown-ups' store.

BOOKS OF WONDER
132 Seventh Ave.	212-989-3270
464 Hudson	212-645-8006

7 days

One visit should hook kids on books forever; you'll see new titles, classics, first editions and (on 7th Ave.) one of the largest collections anywhere of Oz books.

CREATIVE BEGINNINGS
PERSONALIZED CHILDREN'S BOOKS
914-964-6745
914-965-0467
Mon.-Fri.

How's this for realism: this source will make your one-to-eight-year-old the star in illustrated books, from teddy bear birthdays to dinosaur adventures.

EEYORE'S BOOKS
FOR CHILDREN
25 E. 83rd St.
212-988-3404

2212 Broadway
212-362-0634
7 days

Miniature wonderlands that keep kids enchanted with booksignings, magic shows, and storytelling. Well-informed staff, fascinating classics make it a treat for grown-ups, too.

BOOKS—Comics & Magazines

ACTION COMICS
318 E. 84th St.
212-249-7344
7 days

Faster than a speeding bullet, old comic books have skyrocketed in value. Action buys, sells, and displays some of the rarest. You'll also find base-

ball cards and collector's supplies like boxes and
plastic sheets.

A & S BOOK COMPANY
304 W. 40th St.
212-695-4987, 212-714-2712
Mon.-Sat.
No c.c.

*For research or just nostalgia, check A & S for
back issues of every possible periodical; they specialize in old cinema, sports, and fashion magazines.*

DELTA PUBLISHING GROUP
1-800-SAVE-SAVE
7 days

*This clearinghouse saves you half, sometimes
more, on magazine subscriptions, without those
contests and gimmicks; their catalog includes
nearly every major title.*

FORBIDDEN PLANET
821 Broadway
212-473-1576

227 E. 59th St.
212-751-4386
7 days

*Comics have become serious art, and this place
carries all the major and independent editions,
along with horror/sci-fi books, videos, t-shirts.*

JAY-BEE MAGAZINES
134 W. 26th St.
212-675-1600
Mon.-Sat.

Their annual catalog must rank as one of the world's most comprehensive sources for magazine collectors; it includes some of 2 million back issues dating far back as a century.

JIM HANLEY'S UNIVERSE
126 W. 32nd St.   212-268-7088

166 Chambers St.   212-349-2930

350 New Dorp Lane,
Staten Island   718-351-6299
7 days

Probably every comic book and graphic novel in the universe, along with related games, t-shirts, posters, and models; very knowledgeable staff.

MAGAZINE CENTER
1133 Broadway
212-929-5255
Mon.-Fri.

Vintage fashion and men's magazines dating back, it seems, to the dawn of time; if they don't stock it, they'll find it.

MANHATTAN COMICS & CARDS
228 W. 23rd St.
212-243-9349
7 days

Manhattan's oldest comic store caters to serious collectors of vintage comic books and sports trading cards; they also discount new comics up to 30% off cover.

SEE HEAR
59 E. 7th St.
212-505-9781
7 days

For anyone serious about popular and alternative music, this is the place to find magazine, fanzines, and comics; there's also an unbelievable back catalog of vintage rock magazines from the '60s, '70s, and '80s.

BOOKS — General

A PHOTOGRAPHER'S PLACE
133 Mercer St.
212-431-9358
7 days

Every photography book you can picture, including many out-of-print selections.

APPLAUSE THEATER AND CINEMA BOOKSTORE
211 W. 71st St.
212-496-7511
7 days

Actors, actresses, and theater-lovers staff this clut-
tered, charming source for plays, textbooks, criti-
cisms, and anthologies; out-of-print titles, too.

ARGOSY BOOK STORE
116 E. 59th St.
212-753-4455
Mon.-Sat.

Just browsing through the front bins of old maps,
prints, and books can take hours; leave time to
peruse the mammoth stock inside.

BARNES & NOBLE BOOKSTORE
1280 Lexington Ave.	(also Broadway at
212-423-9900	82nd Street
7 days	212-362-8835)

Nobody will recognize this Barnes & Noble "super-
store," with a massive selection, expanded hours,
and comfortable library tables and chairs for
browsing.

BIOGRAPHY BOOK SHOP
400 Bleecker St.
212-807-8655
7 days

Cozy West Village shop devoted exclusively to
biographies and related poetry and fiction; if they
can't locate a title, it might not exist.

BROADWAY BOOK STALLS
110th-116th Streets
no c.c.

Weekends, join the Columbia students who browse upper Broadway for books, CDs, records; surprising finds.

BURLINGTON BOOK SHOP
1082 Madison Ave.
212-288-7420
7 days

For extensive current titles, art books, poetry, and backlist paperbacks — and a smart staff to boot — visit this old-fashioned neighborhood favorite.

DAEDALUS BOOKS
1-800-395-2665
Mon.-Fri.

Remaindered book catalog includes many former bestsellers and obscure treasure discounted up to 90%; worth reading just for the lively, literate blurbs.

DOVER PUBLICATIONS
180 Varick St., ninth floor
212-255-3755
Mon.-Fri.
No c.c.

In this drab-looking office, you'll find an unbelievable selection of scholarly books on arts and sciences from architecture to physics.

DRAMA BOOKSHOP
723 7th Ave.
212-944-0595
7 days

Claims to be America's largest performance arts bookstore, with the City's widest selection of dance titles; imports from Great Britain and Australia.

FOUL PLAY
13 8th Ave.
212-675-5115

1465B Second Ave.
212-517-3222
7 days

Huge selection, well-read staff, friendly service: the clues lead to the city's only bookstore for mystery-lovers, and one of the city's best bookstores bar none.

GOTHAM BOOKMART
41 W. 47th St.
212-719-4448
Mon.-Sat.

"Wise Men Fish Here," boasts the sign above the doorway; in a reverent atmosphere, you'll find literature, film, theater, and art tomes, and rarities.

IDEAL BOOK STORE
1125 Amsterdam Ave.
212-662-1909
Mon.-Fri.

Eccentric, cluttered little shop specializing in academic titles, Judaica, Islam, and historical texts; a beloved resource for thrifty Columbia students.

J.N. BARTFIELD
30 W. 57th St.
212-245-8890
Mon.-Sat. (closed Sat. in summer)
No c.c.

Extraordinary leather-bound books, sporting and Western art, bronzes, and atlases. No bargains, but if you're browsing here you probably didn't expect them anyway.

KITCHEN ARTS AND LETTERS
1435 Lexington Ave.
212-876-5550
Mon.-Sat.

Starved for epicurean literature? You'll find more than 6,000 food-and-wine related titles here from around the world. For out-of-print rarities, KAL also operates a no-charge search service.

MILITARY BOOKMAN
29 E. 93rd St.
212-348-1280
Tues.-Sat.

The pen may be mightier than the sword, but books on war, weapons, and aviation — mostly used — dominate this shop.

MURDER, INC.,
2486 Broadway
212-362-8905
7 days

It would be a crime for fans to forego the selection of mysteries, espionage novels, Sherlockiana, and rare/out-of-print editions here.

MYSTERIOUS BOOKSHOP
129 W. 56th St.
212-765-0900
Mon.-Sat.

Take a clue from the name: new, used, and rare mystery and detective books here, including many autographed copies.

N Y KINOKUIYA BOOKSTORE
10 W. 49th St.
212-765-1461
7 days

New York outpost of Japan's biggest bookstore chain carries the largest selection of Japanese-language and culture books this side of Osaka.

PAGEANT PRINT AND BOOK SHOP
109 E. 9th St.
212-674-5296
Mon.-Sat.

A charming vestige of the old East Village, this cluttered shop draws serious bookworms; old books, prints, and maps from as early as the 15th century.

SAMUEL FRENCH
45 W. 25th St., second floor
212-206-8990
Mon.-Fri.

Part of a nearly-vanished New York, French has been publishing plays for 162 years, and stocks more than 5,000 current titles, as well as unusual out-of-print pieces; serious browsers can sit as long as they like at a reading table.

SCIENCE FICTION SHOP
163 Bleecker St.
212-473-3010
Mon.-Sun.

The final frontier for sci-fi fans, with an enormous stock and catalogue of science fiction, fantasy, and horror books; occasional celeb events.

SHAKESPEARE AND COMPANY
2259 Broadway
212-580-7800
Mon.-Fri.

716 Broadway
212-529-1330
Tues.-Sun.

Named after the legendary Left Bank shop, these booklovers' bookstores keep a vast inventory of hot new titles, trade and mass-market paperbacks, classics, offbeat journals, and magazines. Helpful staff, late hours.

STRAND BOOKSTORE
828 Broadway
212-473-1452

90 John St (at Front St.), South St. Seaport
212-809-0875
7 days

Joan & Gerry's Best Buy

The nation's largest used book store. Prepare to spend half a day browsing through 2 million books over 32,000 feet of floor space (at the legendary Broadway store); 1/2-price reviewer's copies of bestsellers.

THEATER BOOKS
1600 Broadway room 1009
212-757-2834
Mon.-Sat.

The play's the thing here, and so are books on every aspect of theater; there's always a good choice of discounted titles.

URBAN CENTER BOOKS
457 Madison Ave.
212-935-3592
Mon.-Sat.

This East Side source for books on architecture stocks what seems like every word ever written on New York design.

BOXES & TRIM

SO-GOOD
28 W. 38th St.
212-398-0236
Mon.-Fri.
no c.c.

Joan & Gerry's Best Buy
Around the holidays, you'll appreciate this ribbon wholesaler's astonishing selection and rock-bottom prices; $10 minimum, but you'll spend it when the season comes.

U.S. BOX CORPORATION
126 Lombardy St.
Brooklyn, N.Y. 11222
718-387-1510
Mon.-Fri.

Joan & Gerry's Best Buy
Every kind of packaging — giftboxes, candy boxes, padded mailing envelopes, shopping bags
— at unbelievable savings. There's a $150 minimum, and discounts vary with volume; split your order with a friend.

BRIDAL
BRIDAL—Accessories

CINDERELLA FLOWER AND FEATHER COMPANY
60 W. 38th St.
212-840-0644
Mon.-Sat.

Joan & Gerry's Best Buy

Boxes of flowers, feathers, sequins, pearls and rhinestones clutter this old-fashioned shop, a terrific source for bridal trimmings.

CROWNING GLORY HEADPIECES
21 A Ridgeway Ave.
White Plains, NY
914-686-9072

For bridal headpieces, this is one of the area's best sources; you'll also find jewelry, purses, and bridal accessories. They customize shoes and bags, too.

DIANE WAGNER
212-663-1079
By appointment only

You've seen her exquisite bridal headpieces and floral bouquets in <u>Modern Bride</u> and Laura Ashley stores; she can custom-design them for you, too.

GIAN PICO
195 Clarke Ave.
Staten Island, NY
718-8987-3391
Mon.-Fri. by appointment only
No c.c.

He works privately for Kleinfeld, but you can visit this master milliner yourself for a beautiful custom bridal headpiece, his business for 55 years.

LA SPOSA VEILS
8207 Fifth Ave.
Brooklyn, N.Y. 11209
718-680-9665
Tues.-Sat.

252 W. 40th St.
212-354-4729
Mon.-Sat.

Joan & Gerry's Best Buy
In Brooklyn, you'll find a boutique specializing in custom veils, with exquisite lingerie and shoes; their Manhattan location, a fabric store, does beautiful custom veilwork.

M & J TRIMMING
1008 Ave. of the Americas   212-391-6968

1014 Ave. of the Americas   212-391-8731
(trimming for furniture only)

Joan & Gerry's Best Buy
Terrific prices on bridal headpieces, veils, and accessories, as well as every imaginable button, bead, lace, rhinestone, fringe, pearl, feathers.

MANNY'S MILLINERY
SUPPLY COMPANY
26 W. 38th St.   212-840-2235
Mon.-Sat.

Joan & Gerry's Best Buy

A great garment district source for wholesale prices on bulk hats, trimmings, flowers, bridal headpieces, gloves, lace, hatpins, floral sprays, ribbons, veiling, and feathers. Do-it-yourselfers, take note: Combs cost $3/dozen here, and flowers to decorate them start at only 50 cents each. They also custom-design hats.

SHERU ENTERPRISES
49 W. 38th St.
212-730-0766/F: 212/840-2368
Mon.-Sat.

Joan & Gerry's Best Buy

Though officially a wholesaler, Sheru bills itself as "browser's paradise," and they're right; in their bridal department, you'll find a huge selection of accessories and marcasite. Mail order department ships all over the world.

BRIDAL — Gowns

THE BRIDAL BUILDING
1375 and 1385 Broadway
Sat. 10-2

Joan & Gerry's Best Buy

Sneak in early on a Saturday and ask the elevator operator who's open. You may gain access to some of the leading bridal manufacturers. One caveat:

*shop here **only** if you know established retail prices.*

THE DESIGNER'S ROOM
5 Sunrise Plaza
Valley Stream, N.Y.   516-561-5761
Mon.-Fri. by appointment only
No c.c.

Joan & Gerry's Best Buy
Unless they check the label, no one will know you're wearing an Iris Reina clone of a designer wedding gown. Bring in a photo; she'll create a copy.

ELENY'S
Woodbury Plaza, So. Oyster Bay Rd.
Plainview, LI.
516-822-4204
Mon.-Sat. by appointment only

Her custom-designed bridal gowns have drawn raves at weddings we've attended; she also designs suits and casual wear.

I. KLEINFELD AND SON
8202 Fifth Ave.
Brooklyn, N.Y. 11209
718-833-1100

8209 Third Ave
Brooklyn, N.Y. 11209
718-238-1500
Tues.-Sat.

America's most famous bridal source! Rich and poor, famous and not-so-famous, they gather at this local legend for that once-in-a-lifetime gown, wonderful evening wear, cocktail dresses, and flower girl outfits. A bridal consultant can help you navigate through over a thousand designs. Call for an apppointment.

JEAN HOFFMAN AND JANA STARR ANTIQUES
236 E. 80th St.   212-535-6930
Mon.-Sat.
Closed Sat. in summer

Perfectly preserved vintage bridal dresses from the turn of the century to the fifties; not cheap, but real originals. Antique clothes, pocketbooks, hats, and jewelry, and stunning antique lace. Prices start at $300; excellent alterations.

OUTLET OF THE BRIDAL CENTER
381 Sunrise Highway
Lynbrook, NY 11563
516-599-8556
Tues.-Sat.

Joan & Gerry's Best Buy
Brides on a budget will find one-of-a-kind designer bridal samples for $200 and under; bridesmaids' dresses, accessories and gown rentals too.

PATRICIA
534 West Side Ave.
Jersey City, N.J. 07304
201-433-1884
Mon.-Sat.
No c.c.

Joan & Gerry's Best Buy

In love with a $3,000 gown in a bridal magazine, but hate the price? Patricia can "recreate" it for a fraction of retail. Custom gowns from around $200; sample gowns for as low as $50.

PEGGY PETERS
213 Middle Neck Road
Great Neck, NY
516-466-8480
Mon.-Sat.

Head to the suburbs for fabulous bridal and bridesmaids' gowns from names like Warter, Dessey, Victor Costa, Scaasi, Jim Helm, Galina, Marisa, Diamond, Elegance, Italia, Caroline Herrera, Paula Varsalona; this place also has the biggest European names like Genny, Louis Feraud, Mila Schon, Zandra Rhodes, Hanae Mori at competitive prices. Watch for twice-yearly sales; tell them we sent you.

PIMENTEL BRIDALS
155 E. 29th St.
212-683-1639
by appointment only

Joan & Gerry's Best Buy

Serious atmosphere lets customers know they're shopping for a Very Important Occasion; classy bridal and evening wear starts at $500, rents for less.

ROSEN AND CHADEK
246 W. 40th St.
212-869-0142
Mon.-Sat.

Joan & Gerry's Best Buy

If you really want to save on a bridal gown, find fabrics here — like beaded lace and European silks — and let a salesperson recommend a custom dressmaker to stitch your dreams together.

RK BOUTIQUE
2276 Broadway
212-362-9512
Mon.-Sat.

Joan & Gerry's Best Buy

One of the city's best bargain sources for prom and party dresses; except for bridal gowns, most outfits cost less than $200; some confirmation dresses as low as $70.

STATUS
747 Fulton St.
Brooklyn, NY 11217
718-596-6333
Mon.-Sat.

Joan & Gerry's Best Buy

So you saw a gorgeous bridal gown, but the price makes you consider staying single? These people can copy any design for a fraction of retail.

VERA WANG BRIDAL HOUSE, LTD.
991 Madison Ave.
212-628-3400
Mon.-Sat.
by appointment only

Ultra-exclusive bridal salon features their own collection and designers like Carolina Herrera and Scaasi, with dazzling accessories to match. It pays to wait to get married around their spectacular sales, with unbelievable markdowns on their exquisite dresses. Make sure you get on their mailing list.

VERA WANG MADE-TO-ORDER
Mark Hotel
25 E. 77th St., third floor
212-879-1700

If money's no object, come here for custom evening dresses; you'll get quality work to rival some of the European couture houses.

BRIDAL — Rental

ANTIQUES AT TRADERS COVE
230 Traders Cove
Port Jefferson, LI.
516-331-2261
Tue.-Sat.
No c.c.

Joan & Gerry's Best Buy
For brides, they rent luxurious antique dresses and newer knockoffs at reasonable rates; for

bridal parties, they create outfits to match the wedding theme; for receptions, they decorate with fanciful period props.

ENCHANTING ALTERNATIVES
1860 Wantaugh Ave.
Wantaugh Village, LI
516-785-1430
Wed.-Mon.

Joan & Gerry's Best Buy

Well-priced rentals of bridal gowns ($200-$450), mother-of-the-bride dresses ($40-$150), cocktail dresses ($40-60), prom gowns.

GENE LONDON
897 Broadway
212-533-4105
By appointment only
No c.c.

Joan & Gerry's Best Buy

London rents spectacular bridal and special-occasion dresses; his clients include many movie-star and celebrity brides. He periodically sells off thousands of garments from film and TV productions for a fraction of cost..

ISLAND BRIDAL GOWN RENTAL
148 Broadway
Route 107, Hicksville, LI.
516-681-5816
Tues.-Sat.
No c.c.

Joan & Gerry's Best Buy

Much more than the name implies; on top of renting gowns and headpieces, they alter any gown and restore antique wedding dresses.

JUST ONCE LTD.
292 Fifth Ave., third floor
212-465-0960
Mon.-Fri.

Joan & Gerry's Best Buy

Why spend a fortune on formal clothes you'll wear once? For a fraction of what they cost, you can rent fabulous Carolina Herrera, Scaasi, and Diamond Collection gowns and wedding dresses here.

BRIDAL — Shoes

FANCY FOOTWORK
718-855-4592
by appointment only

For bridal party shoes and custom evening shoes, try this reliable source; designer Susan Feingold does meticulous handbeading and decorating.

PETER FOX
378 Amsterdam Ave   212-874-8899

105 Thompson St.   212-481-6359
7 days

Come to them with any idea for bridal shoes, no matter how wild, and they'll do it; they'll also turn any of their own whimsical designs into bridal shoes.

VAMPS
1421 Second Ave.
212-744-0227
7 days

Joan & Gerry's Best Buy

*If you could just dye your bridal party's shoes,
bring them here; there's a 24-hour dye service and
10% discount for orders of four shoes or more.
Good prices on top-name shoes, too.*

BRIDAL — Special Sizes

LARGE AND LOVELY
381 Sunrise Highway
Lynbrook, LI

Joan & Gerry's Best Buy

*Larger-size women who've had trouble finding
stylish bridalwear should drop by this place; you
can try on gowns in sizes 18-56.*

BUTTONS

GORDON BUTTON COMPANY
222 W. 38th St.
212-921-1684
Mon.-Fri.
No c.c.

Joan & Gerry's Best Buy

*A button wholesaler since 1925, Gordon now
retails too. Mammoth inventory includes hundreds of wood, metal, rhinestone, and pearl
designs. The store even dyes buttons to match.*

TENDER BUTTONS
143 E. 62nd St.   212-758-7004
Mon.-Sat.
Closed Sat. in July and August
No c.c.

Even if you don't need a button, drop by this tiny, charming shop. Every type of modern and antique button, along with the largest collection of men's antique and new blazer buttons anywhere. New: Button-shaped cookies.

CARPETS/RUGS & FLOOR COVERINGS

ABC CARPET AND HOME
888 Broadway
212-473-3000
7 days

New Yorkers rush here first for almost anything for the home; huge assortment of broadloom, bed and bath accessories, furniture, antiques, at fair prices. Always check the basement for remnants — and ask about their warehouse in the Bronx.

CENTRAL CARPET
426 Columbus Ave.
212-362-5485
7 days

Joan & Gerry's Best Buy
Real bargains on Oriental rugs and carpets, their main business; you'll also find more than 8,000 carpet styles at a discount.

LOVELIA ENTERPRISES
356 E. 41st St.
212-490-0930
Mon.-Fri. by appointment only
No c.c.

A one-woman trade secret for tapestries and miniature rugs, Lovelia Albright imports exquisite European Gobelin, Aubusson, and Beauvais designs for less than anywhere else.

RUG TOWER
399 Lafayette St.
212-677-2525
7 days

Five floors of new and antique oriental rugs and kilims; don't be afraid to bargain.

RUG WAREHOUSE
220 W. 80th St.
212-787-6665
Mon.-Sun.

Joan & Gerry's Best Buy
What it lacks in glamour, it makes up in price and selection. You'll find nearly 3,000 new and used oriental rugs priced very low, and a helpful staff.

SANDLER AND WORTH
800-2-SANDLER

Shops scattered across the tri-state area stock every species of carpet, from basic rugs to exotic orientals; shop-at-home service.

TURKANA GALLERY
125 Cedar St.
212-732-0273
By appointment only
No c.c.

More artworks than accessories, the Middle Eastern kilims here comprise one of the finest collections anywhere. If you don't know the market, bring someone who does.

CHRISTMAS ITEMS

JAMES A. COLE
41 W. 25th St.
212-741-1500
Mon.-Fri.; call for Sat. hours
(holiday season only)
No c.c.

This cheerful Toy District source supplies the department stores and retailers with Christmas trees, lights, ornaments, garlands, and holiday props; open to the public late October / early November, after retailers have had their pick. You're buying leftovers, but who'll know?

CLOTHING

CLOTHING — Accessories

AMALGAMATED
19 Christopher St.
212-691-8695
7 days

Very cool hats, belts, shoes, and tops from Stussy, Basco, Artichoke Design are for men, but women love them too; this tiny "compartment store" also manages to squeeze in jewelry and accessories.

EAST VILLAGE LEATHER
27 St. Marks Place
212-533-8330
7 days

Now that biker chic has even hit Uptown, this is the place for authentic, affordable motorcycle jackets, boots, and belts.

FINE AND KLEIN
119 Orchard St.
212-674-6720
Sun.-Fri.
No c.c.

Joan & Gerry's Best Buy

On three floors, Fine and Klein stocks a huge array of designer bags, wallets, umbrellas, and belts at discounts up to 35%; a must on any Lower East Side shopping expedition.

HOUSE
84 E. 7th St.
212-677-7379
7 days

Joan & Gerry's Best Buy

Up-to-the-second, very cheap "street"-inspired caps, t-shirts, and accessories; mostly for youngsters, but we've seen women jazz up designer outfits with this stuff.

J.S. SUAREZ
26 W. 54th St.
212-315-5614
Mon.-Sat.

Joan & Gerry's Best Buy

In this neighborhood, you don't call them knock-offs; these bags are "unlabeled" "Hermes," "Chanel," "Celine," and "Botega Veneta" for about half what the real thing costs.

MICHAEL KLEIN'S FOMO
61 Orchard St.
212-925-6363
Sun.-Fri.

Son of renowned leathergoods family sells import-ed Courreges, Carlos Falchi, Cosci bags, belts, wallets up to half off retail; FOMO = "Finally on My Own."

SCHMOOZ
317 Grand St.
212-925-6363
Sun.-Fri.

Joan & Gerry's Best Buy

Lower East Side discounts on trendy Uptown shoes, bags, belts, and wallets; names like Kenneth Cole, Nicole Mulce, Carlos Falchi, and Cosci of Italy.

CLOTHING — Children's

A&G INFANTS & CHILDREN'S WEAR
261 Broome St.
212-966-3775
Sun.-Fri.
(closed on Fri. an hour before sundown)

Joan & Gerry's Best Buy

Name-brand kidswear discounted at least 25% off retail; you'll find brands like Tickle Me % Tackle Me, Crazy Lady, Young Gallery, Choozie.

BEN'S FOR KIDS
1380 Third Ave.
212-794-2330
Mon.-Sat.

Friendly neighborhood source for baby needs, from toys and clothes to furniture and accessories.

IDEAL DEPARTMENT STORE
1814-16 Flatbush Ave.
Flatbush, Brooklyn
718-252-5090
Mon.-Sat.

One of the only sources in the City for Boy and Girl Scout supplies and school uniforms; they deliver everywhere.

KIDS PLUS
70 Highway 10 (Westbound lane)
Whippany, NJ 07981
201-386-1005
Mon.-Sat.

Joan & Gerry's Best Buy

Really a wholesaler, this place offers tremendous discounts on names like Osh Kosh, Bugle Boy, Levi's, and Tickle Me; sizes to 14 for girls, 20 for boys.

LEONIE POWER
1735 Madison Place
Brooklyn, NY 11229
718-339-3540
By Appointment Only

Exquisite christening and prom dresses in classic styles from $200; lots of Victorian lace, ruffles, and roses, so fashion slaves should look elsewhere.

RICE & BRESKIN
323 Grand St.
212-925-5515
Sun.-Fri.

Joan & Gerry's Best Buy

Three floors of bargains in kids' clothing, infants to size 14, from names like Carter's, Healthtex, Dorissa Dress, Renzo, Rothschild.

RISING STAR
459 Mt. Pleasant Ave.
West Orange, NJ 07052
201-736-4224
Mon.-Fri.

Special-occasion and party dresses for young ladies, as well as custom designs for hard-to-fit preteen and teen sizes.

YOUNG ELEGANCE
433 Chesnut Ridge Rd. (Tice Farms)
Woodcliff Lake, NJ 07675
201-930-0949
Mon.-Sat.

So your little girl wants a choice? How about 13 dress lines with over 100 custom samples — and inventory from 100 manufacturers to boot? Worth the trip.

CLOTHING — Men's Custom Tailored

ARGYLE CUSTOM CLOTHIER
PO Box 352
Brelle, NJ 08730
1-800-727-9665 (call for brochure)

Too busy to shop for clothes? Order in. Argyle's tailors will visit your home or office and create impeccable custom suits, shirts, ties, underwear, even shoes.

ARTHUR GLUCK
37 W. 57th St.
212-755-8165
7 days
No c.c.

Mega-exclusive Midtown men's shirt source; custom shirts in sumptuous fabrics like Sea Island cotton and silk from $170.

CHIPP
342 Madison Ave., 2nd floor
212-687-0850
By appointment

If you don't have a castle or title, you'll feel like it after ordering clothes from here; exquisite custom suits, jackets, even riding clothes at stratospheric prices.

CHRIS-ARTO CUSTOM SHIRT COMPANY
39 W. 32nd St., 6th floor
212-563-4455
Mon.-Fri.
No c.c.

You can choose from more than 500 fabrics here, and the prices won't send you into shock.

DUHAMELL
437 Park Ave. South
212-684-1300
By appointment

If you've just inherited a fortune and want to spend it quick, order custom shirts, pyjamas, or leather apparel from here; impeccable work, sumptuous fabrics.

GILIBERTO DESIGNS
142 W. 36th St., 8th floor
212-685-4925
Mon.-Sat.

Dozens of tailors toil in the background as scores of men take fittings for custom suits, jackets, tuxes, overcoats, and shoes; they can also knock off any garment. Suits from $600, shirts from $68, ties from $40.

HONG KONG CUSTOM TAILORS
72 Narrows Road, South
Staten Island, NY 10305
718-447-7653
By appointment only
No c.c.

Doctors may have ended house calls, but these people still come to your home or office for fittings; they're known for sharp suits in gorgeous fabrics.

HOUSE OF MAURIZIO
18 E. 53rd St.
212-759-3230
By appointment only
No c.c.

Flawless custom suits start at — ready? — $3,000, and go up to who knows where; beautiful ready-made blazers, coats, and suits cost slightly less.

MARK CHRISTOPHER
OF WALL ST.
87 Nassau St.
212-608-0921
26 Broadway
212-509-2355
Mon.-Fri.; Sat., Sun. by appt. only

For boardroom jockeys and Wall St. wannabes, this place has custom suits (from $700) and shirts (from $125) at lower-than-Uptown prices.

NICKY BELLANI
718-447-7653, 718-447-7654
No c.c.

If you're too busy (or lazy) to shop, Bellani will drop by your office or home to fit you for custom suits and shirts; less-than-customary prices.

CLOTHING — Men's Formal

BARRY'S FORMALWEAR
315 Monroe St.
Passaic, NJ 07055
800-648-0116 (sales, ext. 12;
rentals, ext. 28)
Mon.-Sat.

Joan & Gerry's Best Buy

At least 30-60% off retail on tux names like Perry Ellis, Ralph Lauren, Christian Dior, and Pierre Cardin; used tuxedos in colors start at $10, $79 for black.

EISENBERG AND EISENBERG
85 Fifth Ave.
212-627-1290
7 days

Joan & Gerry's Best Buy

Good selection of men's dress and casual clothes,

*but discount formalwear's the real reason to come;
you'll find tuxes and accessories from names like
Perry Ellis, Ralph Lauren, Pierre Cardin, Dimitri,
Bill Blass, Lord West.*

TUXEDO LIQUIDATORS
2 E. 14th St.
212-691-0502

Joan & Gerry's Best Buy

*Forget about renting formalwear — it costs the
same to buy a top-of-the-line tux here. For about
$100, you'll find all-wool models from Dior, Yves
St. Laurent, After Six, Pierre Cardin, pre-rented
but in great condition. Who'll know?*

CLOTHING — Men's General

G & G INTERNATIONAL
62 Orchard St.
212-431-4530
Sun.-Fri.

Joan & Gerry's Best Buy

*Some big menswear names have found their way
down here; you'll find discounted styles from San
Remo, Principe, Geoffrey Beene.*

GILCREST CLOTHES COMPANY
900 Broadway
212-254-8933
7 days

Joan & Gerry's Best Buy

For less than the department stores, you'll find

menswear names like Perry Ellis, Lanvin, and Ralph Lauren suits, shirts, outerwear.

GORSART
9 Murray St.   212-962-0024

10 E. 44th St.   212-557-0200
Mon.-Sat. (closed Sat. in July and Aug.)

Joan & Gerry's Best Buy

Bankers and lawyers flock to this enormous loft for Uptown suits, sportswear, and Alden shoes at Downtown prices; sizes from 36 short to 50 extralong. One of the very best.

LOUIS BARALL AND SON
58 Lispenard St.
212-226-6195
Mon.-Sat. (closed Sat. in July and Aug.)

Joan & Gerry's Best Buy

A secret source for traditional men's clothing at 1/3 off list price; for more than 80 years, savvy Wall Streeters have quietly built business wardrobes from here.

L.S. MEN'S CLOTHING
19 W. 44th St., ste 403
212-575-0933
Sun.-Fri.

Joan & Gerry's Best Buy

One of the few Midtown discount sources for $600-$800 men's suits; natural- and soft-shoulder styles, American brands, and special tuxedo orders.

MARK DOWN MENSWEAR
339 Park Ave. So.
212-982-7731
Mon.-Sat.

Joan & Gerry's Best Buy

Even men who hate shopping will love the discounts here on dress and casual clothes from Ralph Lauren, Cross Creek, Stanley Blacker, and Christian Dior; particularly good buys on sportswear.

NORMAN HILTON
35 E. Elizabeth Ave.
Linden, NJ 07036
908-486-2610
Mon.-Fri.

Joan & Gerry's Best Buy

Exquisite, top-of-the-line hand-made suits you've seen in all the top stores; you can't just walk in here, but they hold a famous factory sale twice a year where you can save 50% off retail. Call for dates and hours, and make sure to get your name on their mailing list.

PARK KENNY
920 Broadway
Third floor
212-477-1948
7 days

Joan & Gerry's Best Buy

High-quality shirts, ties, coats that would look at home on Wall St.; fine fabrics distinguish their suit selection.

PARKWAY N.Y.
12 Gold St.   212-809-6636
Mon.-Fri.

30 Vesey St.   212-962-7500
Mon.-Sat.

*High-end traditional outerwear and accessories at
50% off retail from names like Manhattan, Botany
500, Polo, Chaps, Perry Ellis, Bill Blass, London
Fog, Gant.*

SAINT LAURIE
897 Broadway   212-473-0100
7 days

*Real people, not machines, actually craft the tradi-
tional suits, sport jackets, and slacks at this vener-
able-but-hip family-owned outlet; very realistic
prices.*

SEEWALDT & BAUMAN
17 W. 45th St.   212-682-3958
Mon.-Fri.
No c.c.

*From impeccable imported fabrics, this men's
clothier custom-designs very sharp, solid, conservative shirts.*

TOBALDI HUOMO
83 Rivington St.
212-260-4330
Sun.-Thurs.

*Some of the Italian labels here we've never heard
of, but look carefully and you'll find some big-
name shoes and sweaters.*

W. WEBER AND COMPANY
22 W. 21st St.   212-255-6630
By appointment only
No c.c.

Joan & Gerry's Best Buy

This men's clothing importer takes appointments for private customers. Traditional slacks, sport-coats, and overcoats from Eastern European and domestic sources look solid and cost much less than retail.

CLOTHING—Women's Custom Tailored

ACCOMPLICE
529 Broome St.
212-431-6931
Tues.-Sat. by appointment

Carnaby St. meets the Renaissance in Soho; pricy, hippie-trippy custom clothes in sumptuous fabrics.

GHOST TAILOR
34 E. 7th St.
212-995-0092
by appointment only
no c.c.

Joan & Gerry's Best Buy

Bring designer Jean Suchorsky a favorite dress or coat. She'll get rid of unnecessary details, add practical touches like pockets or warmer linings, and improve the fit of the original; very reasonable prices for impeccable work.

ILANA DESIGNS
212-570-9420
By appointment only
No c.c.

Joan & Gerry's Best Buy

Most of Ilana's clients need "missing pieces" of their wardrobes, like suits or blouses they can't find in their size; this top-secret source also duplicates designers like Armani, Lacroix, and Vicky Tiel.

JON HAGGINS
306 W. 38th St.
212-563-2570
by appointment only

Not a knockoff house, this place crafts custom evening and special-occasion dresses from $700; they use their own designs only.

MANDANA
1175 Lexington Ave.
212-988-0800
Mon.-Fri.

Joan & Gerry's Best Buy

This place translates Galanos, Armani, and Ungaro into affordable lookalikes; using their fabric, a Chanel-like suit, including skirt and jacket, will run around $1,200. If you think that's a lot, check price tags on the real thing.

ONE-OF-A-KIND
134 1/2 E. 62 St.
212-832-2152, 212-371-4842
Mon.-Sat.

Joan & Gerry's Best Buy

Bring photos or sketches of high-ticket designer clothes; you'll get a line-for-line copy hard to tell from the original. A "Chanel" suit in wool crepe can cost $1,000; two-piece "Chanel" dress in silk georgette with signature bows, $1,500; "Genny" suit in silk faille, $1,000. They'll clone any designer.

CLOTHING — Women's General

AGI BROOKS
192 Spring St.
212-431-4717
7 days

Local designer offers glamourous, tres *European shirts and tailored suits for women.*

AN ANGELHEART STORE
410 Columbus Ave.
212-496-6170
7 days

Pretty, delicate-looking shop has pretty, delicate-looking clothes with a difference — everything's unfussy and oversized.

COLIN BAER DESIGNS
76 E. 7th St.
212-677-5000
Tues.-Sun.
no c.c.

East Seventh St. has become Seventh Ave. with an attitude, showcasing exciting new work from local designers; Baer's among the best, with pretty tailored women's clothes that boast subtle, daffy details.

DARRYL'S
488-490 Amsterdam Ave.
212-874-6677
7 days

Professional staff can help you edit a whole wardrobe from the beautifully tailored European clothes here; expensive, but terrific values for the price point.

HALO
96 E. 7th St.
212-614-9714
7 days

Simple, relaxed, near-perfect women's clothes with an unpretentious Downtown flavor.

J. MORGAN PUETT
527 Broome St.
212-274-9586
Tues.-Sat.

Roomy, very unusual linen dresses and overalls; worth a look for its striking interior.

JOANIE JAMES NY
117 E. 7th St.
212-505-9653
7 days

*Small shop with slim styles for skinny people;
worth a look for original Lycra dresses, hand-tai-
lored suits. Skip dessert for a week before walking
in here.*

THE LOFT
141 W. 36th St.
212-736-3358
Mon.-Sat.

Joan & Gerry's Best Buy
*For 30-40% off retail, you'll find top-of-the-line
designer sportswear here by the names you always
see in fashion magazines — like Donna Karan —
in sizes 2-14.*

MS., MISS OR MRS.
(*also known as Ben Farber*)
212 W. 35th St.
Fifteenth Floor
212-736-0557
Mon.-Sat.

Joan & Gerry's Best Buy
*Browse at the department stores, then come here to
buy — you'll find some of the priciest Seventh Ave.
labels, at least 30% off retail. You're assigned a
salesperson the minute you walk in, and you'll
appreciate them as they guide you through a huge
inventory of dressier items.*

SHULIE'S
175 Orchard St.
212-473-2480
Sun.-Fri.

Joan & Gerry's Best Buy

You've seen Tahari's sleek, sexy suits and dresses in Uptown stores; you'll find them here half-price. Insiders say the owner is Tahari's sister.

SIMPLY SAMPLES
150 W. 36th St.
212/268-0448
Mon.-Fri

When they don't want to deal with department stores, some of the best Seventh Avenue manufacturers drop clothes at this place; it's like finding a fabulous, private clearance sale. We found a $350 wool blazer from a design superstar, and a $195 white silk organza blouse by a name you'd recognize, for $25 apiece. Call first; you never know what you'll find.

TAMARA
134 E. 70th St.
212-628-0902
Mon.-Fri.

You'd never know from the outside, but this store is a terrific source for knits and French originals. Recent finds include seductive Steve Fabrikant designs for $400-$500, and Adolfo pieces in the $900 range.

WILLOW
353 Amsterdam Ave.
212-496-7764
7 days

*Clothes as delicate as the name; Balinese silks,
patchwork kimono vests, hand-painted velvets,
and gorgeous jewelry and accessories from around
the world.*

CLOTHING — Men's & Women's

CENTURY 21
22 Cortlandt St.
212-227-9092
Mon.-Sat.

*Gaultier, Gigli, Dolce & Gabbana, Byblos,
Versace, Katharine Hamnett, Moschino, Armani,
Polo, Timberland, Joan & David, Zodiac, more —
the real thing, all up to half off retail, sometimes
even cheaper. Discount appliances, linens, fragrances, electronics, kitchen utensils, too. You'll
never want to pay retail again.*

CHEAP & CHIC
81 Third Ave.
212-995-2395
7 days

"Cheap" describes how this place looks from outside, but on good days you'll find chic samples and overstocks from Basco, C.P. Company, and Moschino inside.

DAFFY'S FIFTH AVE.
Fifth Ave. and 18th St.
212-529-4477
7 days

Joan & Gerry's Best Buy
At this discount retailer of men's, women's, and kidswear, the chrome racks sometimes carry names like Byblos, Vittadini, Perry Ellis, Polo, and Anne Klein.

DOLLAR BILL'S
99 E. 42nd St.
212-867-0212
Mon.-Sat.

Joan & Gerry's Best Buy
They almost hustled us out when we started writing names down, so trust us: you'll see designer labels you recognize from exclusive stores up to half off retail. Men's and women's suits, casualwear, sunglasses; rumor has it they hold the best stuff in a fabled back room for loyal customers.

FLEISCHER
186 Orchard St.
212-228-6980

For Men:
183 Orchard St.
212-473-1380
Sun.-Fri.

Joan & Gerry's Best Buy
Call it Russian Roulette shopping; poking through racks here can yield big-name labels on good days, junk on others.

FRIEDLICH
96 Orchard St.
212-254-8899
Sun.-Fri.; closed Tues.

Patience and persistence pay off here with names like Bill Blass, Anne Klein, Dior, and Ralph Lauren at Lower East Side prices; don't take chances on no-name goods.

HARVÉ BENARD
225 Meadowlands Pkwy.
Secaucus, NJ 07096
201-319-9780
7 days

Joan & Gerry's Best Buy
You've seen their sharp suits, sportscoats, and casualwear in the department stores; you'll find them here at 30-60% off retail.

KATINKA
303 E. 9th St.
212-677-7897
Tues.-Sat.
Call as hours may vary
No c.c.

There's no Katinka, but there is Jane Williams, whose dazzling designs in Indian and ethnic cloth draw a star-studded clientele. From Asia and South America, she also imports one-of-a-kind accessories.

NEW REPUBLIC
93 Spring St.
212-219-3005
7 days

Classic meets twisted at this Soho stalwart; traditional shapes, colors, and patterns for men and women impeccably cut into stylish jackets, pants, sweaters, shirts.

NICOLINA
247 W. 46th St.
212-302-6426
7 days

Surprise: At this unique shop hidden in the Theater District's "restaurant row," you'll find eclectic, one-of-a-kind accessories and clothes; we love the 3/4-length jackets made from old Indian blankets for under $200, along with great belts, scarves, and unusual beaded coats and bags. Handsome men's Western shirts, too.

PATRICIA FIELD
408 Sixth Ave.
212-777-1451

10 E. 8th St.
212-254-1699
7 days

Some of the luster has come off these Downtown style emporia, but they're still where some of the hippest kids find nightclubbing outfits; don't miss the makeup and wig counters.

REMINISCENCE
175 MacDougal St.
212-979-9440
7 days

Joan & Gerry's Best Buy

Retro-inspired clothes at retro-inspired prices; there's also a well-chosen selection of vintage clothes.

RESSLER ENTERPRISES
499 Seventh Ave. South, 2nd floor
212-239-7272
no c.c.

Joan & Gerry's Best Buy

These people make the luxurious wool and cashmere coats that end up with pricy designer labels; they open their doors only a few times a year for sample sales that can save you up to 30% off <u>wholesale</u>.

STUSSY
104 Prince St.
212-274-8855
7 days

You might not know if you're over 20, but this skate-and-surf-inspired clothing line has become the hottest thing for hip kids; suggest a visit to their only New York store and teenagers will think you're unbelievably cool.

WEISS & MAHONEY
142 Fifth Ave.
212-675-1367
7 days

A notch above your average army-navy store, this place carries functional flight jackets, fatigues, peacoats, sweaters; you'll also find unusual 1920s apparel relics.

CLOTHING — Hosiery, Lingerie, & Undergarments

A.W. KAUFMAN
73 Orchard St.,   212-226-1629

74 Fifth Ave.   212-243-2922
Sun.-Fri.

Joan & Gerry's Best Buy
Some of the same sleepwear you'll find uptown, discounted deeply; loungewear, sleepwear, camisole sets, cashmere and wool robes, slippers.

ASIATIC HOSIERY COMPANY
195 Paterson Ave.
P.O. Box 31
Little Falls, NJ 07424
1-800-899-LEGS (within 201 area code,
201-256-7701)

Joan & Gerry's Best Buy

This wholesaler will sell men's and boys socks in minimum quantities of a dozen; if you need to stock up, you won't find cheaper prices. Call for catalog.

BARE NECESSITIES
American Way Mall
Fairfield, N.J.
201-227-8871
Mon.-Sun.

Just about every brand of bra we've ever seen under one roof; look for Maidenform, Bally, Carnival, Lilliane at a discount.

CHAS. WEISS FASHIONS
331 Grand St.
212-966-1143
Sun.-Fri.

Joan & Gerry's Best Buy

The city's largest bra and foundation department, they claim; at Orchard St. prices, you'll also find sleepwear, slips, camisoles, and bathing suits.

D & A MERCHANDISE COMPANY
22 Orchard St.
212-925-4766
Mon.-Fri.

Joan & Gerry's Best Buy
The family that shops for underwear together stays together, and you can do it through this discount emporium; mail-order only, call for catalog.

EISNER BROTHERS
75 Essex St
212-475-6868
Sun.-Fri.

76 Orchard St. (Mail Orders)
Sun.-Fri.
No c.c.

Joan & Gerry's Best Buy
We've never seen as big an assortment of t-shirts anywhere; they mostly sell wholesale, so savings grow with quantity. Sweatshirts and baseball caps too.

EVA TEES
83 Essex St.
212-473-1650
Sun.-Fri.
No c.c.

Joan & Gerry's Best Buy
From all the big names — Hanes, Fruit of the Loom, Lee — you'll find discounted t-shirts, sweatshirts, and jerseys here.

GOLDMAN & COHEN
55 Orchard St.
212-966-0737
Sun.-Fri.

Joan & Gerry's Best Buy
This discounter offers a seemingly endless selection of name-brand ladies' lingerie at least 20% off retail.

JACOB YOUNG AND SON
329 Grand St.
212-925-9232
Sun.-Fri.
No c.c.

Joan & Gerry's Best Buy
Though they mostly imprint t-shirts, you can find very cheap underwear and hosiery here from name brands like Hanes.

JOOVAY
436 W. Broadway
212-431-6386
7 days

Huge selection of delicious lingerie from top names like Hanro, LaPerla, Lejaby; price tags reflect chic Soho location.

L'EGGS BRAND
PO Box 748
Rural Hall, NC 27098
919-744-1790
Mon.-Sat.

Joan & Gerry's Best Buy
Their catalogs — Showcase of Savings or Just My Size for large sizes — take you straight to the source for discounts from brands you'll recognize.

MAJESTIC HOSIERY AND UNDERWEAR
86 Orchard St.
212-473-7990
Sun.-Fri.
no c.c.

Joan & Gerry's Best Buy
These old-fashioned wholesalers sell to retail customers, too; Hanes and other brand-name men's and women's undergarments at prices beyond cheap.

MENDEL WEISS
91 Orchard St.
212-925-6815
Sun.-Fri.

Joan & Gerry's Best Buy
Legendary source for wonderful buys on women's undergarments, t-shirts, activewear; don't expect ambience, but you'll love the old-fashioned bargains.

NATIONAL WHOLESALE COMPANY
400 National Blvd.
Lexington, NC 27294
704-246-5904
Mon.-Sat.

Joan & Gerry's Best Buy
Get your hands on their mail-order catalog for terrific bargains on pantyhose and undergarments.

ROUND-THE-CLOCK PANTY HOSE BY MAIL
800-926-4022
Mon.-Fri.

Joan & Gerry's Best Buy
Not a 24-hour hosiery hotline, but a direct line for 20% off Round-the-Clock and Givenchy pantyhose. Call for a brochure.

ULTRA SMART
15 E. 30th St.
212-686-1564
Mon.-Fri.
No c.c.

Joan & Gerry's Best Buy
Designer stockings without designer labels — or price tags; these people buy hosiery from big mills and sell them under their own label.

UNDER WARES
1098 Third Ave.
212-535-6006; 800/237-8641
7 days

For the truly image-conscious, this place sells more than 100 styles of men's designer underwear and boxer shorts; they claim the world's largest selection of men's undergarments.

UNDERWORLD PLAZA
1421 62nd St.
Brooklyn, N.Y. 11219
718-232-6804
Sun.-Fri.

Joan & Gerry's Best Buy

Not a Mafia shopping mall, but a terrific source for lingerie, discounted up to 75%; impressive selection of bridal peignoir sets and trousseau items.

VALUE HOSIERY
272 Fifth Ave.
Park Slope, Brooklyn
718-499-6721
Sun.-Fri.
no c.c.

Joan & Gerry's Best Buy

If you need to stock up on socks, check out this underwear emporium; you won't find better prices on leotards, bathing suits, dancewear, pantyhose.

WEARABLES INTERNATIONAL APPAREL
P.O. Box 8521
Saddle Brook, NJ 07662
no c.c.

Joan & Gerry's Best Buy

No-name but high-quality hosiery for men, women, kids at cheaper-than-cheap prices; write for their catalog.

CLOTHING — Maternity

DAN HOWARD'S MATERNITY FACTORY
5077 Merrick Road
Massapequa, N.Y. 11762
516-799-1242
Sat.-Thur.

Other locations include Carle Place, Centerreach, and Commack, NY.

Joan & Gerry's Best Buy

Inexpensive nursing aids, lingerie, and, of course, maternity wear; a little money goes a long way here.

PARENT PENDING
1178 Lexington Ave.
212-988-3996
7 days

Mothers-to-be tired of dressing like Bette Davis in <u>Whatever Happened to Baby Jane</u> will find a more fashionable alternative here; maternity clothes for grown-ups with busy lives.

CLOTHING — Special Sizes

MURRAY'S
160-13 Northern Blvd.
Flushing, NY 11358
718-463-6644
Mon.-Sat.

Up to men's size 78, this place carries clothes and shoes in large sizes from designers like Pierre Cardin and Sergio Tacchini; men's and women's, with an especially good selection for children.

CLOTHING — Children's Special Sizes

KIDS AT LARGE
Building 32
Endicott St.
Norwood, MA 02062
617-769-8575
Mon.-Fri.; 24 Hour Mail Order

Relief for large kids and their parents who've found apparel shopping a nightmare; this catalog contains cool clothes for hard-to-fit children ages 4-14.

CLOTHING — Men's Special Sizes

BLAIR
Route 662
Warren, PA 16366
1-800-458-6057

3016 W. Eighth St.
Erie, PA 18417

Everything big men need for their hard-to-put-together wardrobes: suits to size 52, shirts to 18 1/2, pants to waist 48. Outerwear and underwear, too.

IMPERIAL WEAR
48 W. 48th St.
212-719-2590
Mon.-Sat.

Big-name clothes for big and tall men, including Izod Lacoste, Perry Ellis, Bill Blass, London Fog; Bally shoes, too.

KNICKERBOCKER SHOP
370 Knickerbocker Ave.
Brooklyn, NY 11237
718-452-8000
7 days

Big men and husky boys should check here for dressy and casual clothes; they'll find a good selection of shorts, an elusive item in large sizes.

KRUG'S BIG & TALL
16 N. Washington Ave.
Bergenfield, NJ 07621
201-387-0100
Mon.-Sat.

Who says big and tall men can't look fashionable? You'll find names like Adolfo, Nino Cerutti, Bill Blass, Palm Beach here.

ROCHESTER BIG & TALL
1301 Ave. of the Americas
212-247-7500
Mon.-Sat.

One of the world's largest collections of clothing for big men; head-to-toe selection includes sharp suits from Canali, Lubiam, Perry Ellis, and Hickey-Freeman; smart Gant, Levi Docker, Cutter & Buck, and Mondo sportswear; shoes from Bally, Cole-Haan; even underwear. Sizes from 48 regular to 60 extra long.

SHORT SIZES
Southgale Shopping Center
5385 Warrensville Center Rd.
Cleveland, OH 44137
216-475-2515

*Instead of getting frustrated in a department
store, shorter men should call here for a catalog;
smaller-sized dress-, casual-, and sleepwear, shoes
from 5 1/2.*

CLOTHING — Women's
Special Sizes

FORMAN'S PETITE
94 Orchard St.
212-228-2500
Sun.-Fri.

Joan & Gerry's Best Buy
*You'll find mostly no-name womenswear at deep
discounts here; comb carefully for petites from
Liz Claiborne and S.N.Y.*

CLOTHING — Sweaters & Knitwear

BEST OF SCOTLAND
581 Fifth Ave.
212-644-0415
Mon.-Sat.

You'll find the same luxurious cashmere sweaters here you've see in 57th St. shops, without the high-rent price tags.

CASHMERE CASHMERE
840 Madison Ave.
212-988-5252

595 Madison Ave.
212-935-2522
Mon.-Sat.; Sun. near Christmas

Bargain-hunters, stop reading now; ultra-luxurious, private-label cashmere sweaters, dresses, pajamas, slippers, and robes for men, women, and very lucky kids.

DECKERS
666 W. Ave.
So. Norwalk, CT 06850
203-866-5593
7 days

Joan & Gerry's Best Buy

They say they've got the country's largest selection of men's and women's cashmere sweaters, and it looks like it; huge stock of dress shirts and ties, too.

FISHKIN KNITWEAR CO.
314 and 318 Grand St.   212-226-6538
Sun.-Fri.

Joan & Gerry's Best Buy
You'd never guess from the outside, but this place has terrific deals on cashmere sweaters from names like Adrienne Vittadini and Regina Porter.

FRENCH CREEK SHEEP & WOOL COMPANY
Elverson, PA. 19520   215-286-5700
Mon.-Sat.

Their catalog showcases solid shearlings and wool sweaters under their own label only.   Quality on other leathers and suedes looks high; they do alterations.

SCALERA OUTLET
790 Madison Ave., suite 301   212-517-7417
Mon.-Fri.

Gawk at the stunning wool and cashmere knitwear in their store next door; at season's end, come here to buy some of the same pieces at 30-60% off retail.

CLOTHING — Swimsuits

J. CREW CATALOG
800-562-0258
Daily 24 hours
Since they let you order by the piece, this catalog is a great source for bathing suit tops and bottoms in two different sizes.

ROSE MARIE REID OUTLET
3350 Liberty Ave.
North Bergen, NJ 07047
201-867-2020
Sat.-Sun.
(closed from the end of Sept. to the end of winter)

Joan & Gerry's Best Buy

At this huge outlet, much of the Bill Blass, Rose Marie Reid, and Esther Williams swimsuits and sportswear come in at $20 or less; sizes 6-16.

SWIM AND CRUISEWEAR OUTLET
590 Smith St.
Farmingdale, N.Y. 11735
516-420-1400
Thurs., Sat. only
Open March/April through the end of July
No c.c.

Joan & Gerry's Best Buy

The same first-quality women's cruisewear, sportswear, and swimwear you see in department stores, but prices won't push you off the deep end.

YOURS ALONE SWIMWEAR
14 Roosevelt Ave.
Chatham, NJ
201-701-1777
Tues.-Sat.

Swimsuits that look fabulous on models often look less fabulous on us. The solution: a custom bathing suit that flatters where it should. After a computer measurement, you'll have a suit in two weeks. Ideal for mastectomy patients.

CLOTHING — Vintage & Consignment

CANAL JEANS
504 Broadway
212-226-1130
7 days

Joan & Gerry's Best Buy

Twentysomethings flock to this Soho emporium for inexpensive bomber jackets, shoes, jeans, streetwear, and vintage finds. For ultra-cheap bargains, check the bins outside the store; for extra cash, sell your old clothes here.

DOROTHY'S CLOSET
335 Bleecker St.
212-206-6414
7 days

Fun, funky, and friendly, this Village vintage clothing depot specializes in finds from the `30s-`60s.

ENCORE RESALE DRESS SHOP
1132 Madison Ave.
7 days

Joan & Gerry's Best Buy
Some rich and famous ladies unload entire wardrobes here; that means fabulous buys on gently worn designer clothing and accessories on two floors.

EXCHANGE UNLIMITED
563 Second Ave.
212-889-3229
Mon.-Sat.
No c.c.

Joan & Gerry's Best Buy
Some gently used clothing, but the real finds here are one-of-a-kind designer pieces on consignment for a fraction of boutique prices; we found a mint-condition Ungaro jumpsuit.

THE FAMILY JEWELS
832 Sixth Ave.
212-679-5023
7 days

Joan & Gerry's Best Buy
Four decades of vintage clothing stuffed in a postage-stamp-size second-floor shop; gowns, men's coats, used jeans, and more from the '30s-'60s.

GABAY'S
225 First Ave.
212-254-3180
7 days

Joan & Gerry's Best Buy

Feeling adventuresome? Rummage through the overstocks, seconds, and mysterious remnants at this East Village clearinghouse; we found a Valentino Uomo blazer in perfect condition.

GENE LONDON
897 Broadway
212-533-4105
By appointment only
No c.c.

Joan & Gerry's Best Buy

London periodically sells off thousands of garments from film and TV productions for a fraction of cost. He also rents spectacular bridal and special-occasion dresses.

HARRIET LOVE
126 Prince St.
212-966-2280
Tue.-Sun.

Trendy shop with `40s clothes that look new, new clothes that look old, and real antique jewelry, alligator bags, and scarves. Heaven for collectors.

HOUSING WORKS THRIFT SHOP
136 W. 18th St.
212/366-0820
Mon.-Sat.
no c.c.

Joan & Gerry's Best Buy

Here's a worthwhile excuse to go shopping: all the proceeds from this comfortable, convivial second-hand emporium near Barneys go to homeless people with HIV.

INA
101 Thompson St.
212-941-4757
Tues.-Sun.
no c.c.

Second-hand shopping goes upscale; Alaia, Calvin Klein, Versace, Mugler, Donna Karan, Anne-Marie Beretta — all spotted on recent visits — gently worn, for a fraction of their original prices. An absolute must for label fanatics.

MICHAEL'S
1041 Madison Ave., 2nd floor
212-737-7273
Mon.-Sat.

Joan & Gerry's Best Buy

Secondhand Valentino, Calvin Klein, Armani, Ungaro in such good shape you'll think they're new; the rich and famous bring their designer discards here.

ROSE IS VINTAGE
350 E. 9th St. *
212-979-7660

96 E. 7th St.
212-533-8550
7 days
no c.c.

Now that recession chic has hit New York, second-hand clothes have found a new cachet; come here for some of the best, and best-priced.

SCREAMING MIMI'S
22 E. 4th St.
212-677-6464
7 days

Joan & Gerry's Best Buy

Cool collections of hot vintage clothing and young designers keep this East. Village stalwart on the map. If only to see the trippy shoe department — with $5 go-go boots next to $95 platforms — drop in here.

CLOTHING — Western

COMMON GROUND
19 Greenwich Ave.
212-989-4178
7 days

With the Southwestern look as hot as ever, this is the place for authentic Native American jewelry, beaded clothing, and accessories.

KATY K'S
22 E. 4th St.
212-677-6020
7 days

L'il Abner in the E. Village; tongue-in-cheek Western wear from jewelled cowboy shirts and belts to petticoats, gingham skirts, and corsets.

WHISKEY DUST
526 Hudson St.
212-691-5576
7 days

Joan & Gerry's Best Buy

With country music and the two-step becoming this decade's Disco, you can dress the part with second-hand cowboy boots, belts, bandannas, and jeans from this West Village outpost.

COSMETICS & TOILETRIES

THE BATH HOUSE
215 Thompson St.
212-533-0690
7 days

Sweet-smelling store with fabulous all-natural bath oils, bubble baths, body lotions; they also custom-blend fragrances for truly one-of-a-kind perfumes.

BOYD CHEMIST
655 Madison Ave.
212-838-6558
Mon.-Sat.

Sidle up to Boyd's circular cosmetics bar and get primped. When the stylists get through with you, you'll buy more than you wanted, but you'll look better than you thought possible. Fragrances, hypo-allergenic products, optical-quality magnifying mirrors, and a full-service salon inside.

CASWELL-MASSEY CO., LTD.
518 Lexington Ave.   212-755-2254
Mon.-Sat.

21 Fulton St.   212-608-5401
7 days

World Financial Center
225 Liberty St.
7 days   212-945-2630

America's oldest chemist and perfumer, founded in 1752; along with a fascinating history, they carry a superb line of toiletry and personal care items.

KIEHL'S
109 Third Ave.
212-677-3171
Mon.-Sat.

Models, celebs, and mere mortals jockey for attention at the antique counter of this family-owned institution. Very effective, all-natural toners, scrubs, creams, shampoos, and astringents have kept them coming for three generations.

THE MAKE UP CENTER
150 W. 55th St.
212-977-9494
Mon.-Sat.

Make-up Mecca for models and actresses; their own well-priced cosmetics, a full range of theatrical make-up, and reasonable makeovers and skin treatments. Makeup consultants actually take time to help you learn what looks best.

COSMETICS & TOILETRIES —
Perfumes

BIZZARO TURCI
9 E. 17th St.
212-741-1632

THE PERFUME ENCOUNTER
25 E. 17th St.
212-645-8868

Joan & Gerry's Best Buy

JAY'S PERFUME BAR
14 E. 17th St.
212-243-7743

Joan & Gerry's Best Buy

We call it the Fragrance District; in a two-block area, these three sources sell designer fragrances for much less than the department stores.

J.R. TOBACCO
800-JR-CIGAR
11 E. 45th St.
212-983-4160
Mon.-Sat.

219 Broadway
212-233-6620
Mon.-Fri.

36 Route 17 South
Paramus, NJ 07652
201-845-9442
Mon.-Sat.

Joan & Gerry's Best Buy

Well-known tobacco outlet does a lesser-known, but equally huge, business in discount perfume; call 800-JR-CIGAR for order information.

ESSENTIAL PRODUCTS
90 Water St.
212-344-4288
Mon.-Fri

"Interpretations" of designer fragrances for about $18-$25 an ounce, much less than the real thing; they'll even refill original bottles with their concoctions.

PARISIAN PERFUMES
AND COSMETICS
123 Fifth Ave.
212-254-5300

Joan & Gerry's Best Buy
Perfumes you'll recognize at prices close to duty-free.

DECORATING

CALICO CORNERS
323 Route 10
East Hanover, N.J. 07936
201-887-3905
7 days

Joan & Gerry's Best Buy
Enormous selection of first and second-quality fabrics and window treatments; they also offer reupholstering and custom decorating.

DECORATORS WALK OUTLET
141 So. Service Rd.
Plainview, NY 11803
516-249-0003
Mon.-Sat.

Joan & Gerry's Best Buy

You'll find barely-touched floor samples from decorators' showrooms among the discounted furniture, accessories, fabrics, lamps, and mirrors here.

FABRIC ALTERNATIVE
78 Seventh Ave.
Park Slope, Brooklyn
718-857-5482
7 days

An invaluable source for decorating or refurbishing; in beautiful fabrics, they'll custom-sew anything from window treatments to duvet covers for much less than retail.

FORSYTH DECORATORS
100 Forsyth St.
212-226-3624
Sun.-Thurs.
no c.c.

Custom fabric work for window treatments and furniture at much less than the department stores charge; we know people who buy expensive fabric Uptown and bring it here for work.

HEADQUARTERS WINDOWS & WALLS
800-232-6591
7 days

This phone service has terrific prices on wallpaper, fabrics, window treatments, and vertical blinds; know exactly what you want before you call.

INTERCOASTAL TEXTILES
480 Broadway
212-925-9235
Mon.-Sat.

Joan & Gerry's Best Buy

Less-than-wholesale prices on first-class home and upholstery fabrics; unbelievable selection means you'll probably spend hours trying to choose.

L.A. DESIGN CONCEPTS
8811 Alden Dr. Suite 11A
Los Angeles, CA. 90048
310-276-2109
Mon.-Fri.

Joan & Gerry's Best Buy

Imagine you're a decorator who can pay wholesale for the fabulous furniture in <u>Metropolitan Home</u> and <u>House Beautiful</u>. Now open your eyes and call L.A. Design Concepts. For 15% above wholesale cost, they'll purchase and expedite anything sold "to the trade" only; they'll even track down the *fabrics, wallcoverings, lighting, or carpeting you want. Why pay a decorator's markup?*

RICHARD'S INTERIOR DESIGN
1325 Madison Ave.
212-831-9000
7 days

83 Greenwich Ave.
Greenwich, CT 06830
203-622-4300

RICHARD'S ANNEX
234 E. 75th St.
Mon.-Sat.
Joan & Gerry's Best Buy
A one-stop depot for decorating, with decorative fabrics, window treatments, slipcovers, upholstery, wallpapers, and North Carolina furniture. At the Annex, you'll find furniture and fabrics discounted up to half off retail.

SEAPORT FABRICS
Route 27
Mystic, CT. 06355
203-536-8668
Mon.-Sat.
In stock, this place keeps more than 200,000 yards of home decorating fabrics.

STONEHENGE MILL STORE
30 Canfield Rd.
Cedar Grove, N.J. 07009
201-239-9710
Mon.-Sat.

Joan & Gerry's Best Buy
Since Stonehenge does printing for designer upholstery and window fabrics, you can choose stock from different companies; as good as going to the factory.

WEBSTER WALLPAPER
2737 Webster Ave.
212-367-0055
Mon.-Sat.

Joan & Gerry's Best Buy
With more than 2,000 patterns in stock here, you won't have to wait weeks for a particular wallpaper; they'll also customize wallpaper to your fabric.

DECOYS

GROVE DECOYS
36 W. 44th St.
212-391-0688
Tues-Sun

The real thing for decoy lovers. Proprietor William Borden offers basic decoys and one-of-a-kind treasures like early American fish lures. Ducks from $275; fish from $85.

DOMESTICS

AD HOC SOFTWARES
410 W. Broadway
212-925-2652
7 days

Fun, funky household goods imported from around the world; our favorite selection anywhere of the wittiest shower curtains and bathroom accessories.

BED BATH & BEYOND
620 Sixth Ave.
212-255-3550
7 days

Even on roller skates, it would take hours to browse this housewares emporium, the gargantuan Manhattan branch of a national chain; great prices on big-name bathroom, kitchen, bed, patio, office, and kids' items keep it jam-packed, especially on weekends.

BRIDGE KITCHENWARE
214 E. 52nd St.
212-688-4220
Mon.-Sat.

Everything you need for the kitchen, including lots you never knew existed; check out the back room for white restaurant china and terrific serving accessories. Ask for proprietor (and notorious crank) Fred Bridge or son Christopher, who handles the bridal registry.

THE FIELDCREST STORE
Highway 14
Eden, NC 27288
800-841-3336
7 days

Joan & Gerry's Best Buy

You see them in every department store, but you should buy them here; Fieldcrest and Canon towels, comforters, and bedding at deep discounts.

HARRIS LEVY
278 Grand St.
212-226-3102
Sun.-Fri.

One of the Lower East Side's most trusted sources for linens, bedspreads, towels, and drapes; beautiful selection, exquisite custom items.

LA DENTILLIERE
6 Hardwood Court
Scarsdale NY 10583
914-723-2902
Mon.-Sat.

French lace curtains, Italian linens and tableware, gorgeous pillows, and tapestries; since this is Scarsdale, you won't find discounts.

ELECTRONICS

BONDY EXPORT CORPORATION
40 Canal St.
212-925-7785
Sun.-Fri.

Joan & Gerry's Best Buy

Lower East Side discount source has photo equipment, luggage, appliances for 30-50% less than most retailers.

EAST 33RD TYPEWRITER AND ELECTRONICS
42 E. 33rd St.
212-686-0930
7 days

Joan & Gerry's Best Buy

Nothing special on the outside, but terrific bargains inside on fax machines, copiers, computers, and, of course, typewriters; service, too. Ask for Willie. P.S.: Always make sure your purchase comes with a warranty and service guarantee.

FOTO ELECTRIC SUPPLY COMPANY
31 Essex St.
212-673-5222
Sun.-Fri.

Joan & Gerry's Best Buy

Old-fashioned store with the latest Seiko and Casio watches, audio equipment, appliances, cameras, and sunglasses at deep discounts.

GRAND APPLIANCE AND GIFTWARE
335 Grand St.
212-647-3440
Sun.-Fri.

Joan & Gerry's Best Buy

Names like Braun and Eureka don't often turn up at discount electronics places, but they do here; better-than-retail prices on microwaves, clocks, phones, coffee makers, vacuums.

J&R MUSIC WORLD
23 Park Row
212-732-8600
7 days

Up-to-the-minute computers, cameras, radios, televisions, stereos, CD players, tapes and discs, telephones, microwaves, even bread makers fill this electronics "department store." Prices are competitive.

KUNST SALES CORPORATION
45 Canal St.
212-966-1909
Sun.-Fri.

Frequent overseas flyers will appreciate the TVs, stereos, VCRs, and other appliances here; they're all wired for European currents.

RAFIK FILM AND VIDEO TAPE CO.
814 Broadway
212-475-7884
Mon.-Fri.
No c.c.

Though they mostly cater to film and video professionals, this place also sells retail; unbelievable prices on tapes and supplies.

SOUND CITY
58 W. 45th St.
212-575-0210
212-575-1060
Mon.-Sat.

On a street full of electronics outfits, here's one with a difference: professional service, low markup on all major brands of stereo, video, photo, and other home electronics equipment.

TYTELL TYPEWRITER COMPANY
116 Fulton St.
212-233-5333
Mon.-Fri.; by appointment
no c.c.

With two million typefaces in 145 languages and dialects, Tytell's holds the undisputed title of Typewriter Capitol of New York, if not the world; they can repair and restore any machine.

VICMARR STEREO AND TV
88 Delancey St.
212-505-0380, 212-674-9039; F: 212-614-9846
Sun.-Fri.

Low-pressure salespeople; first-rate selection of everything from car audio to camcorders, sunglasses to stereos.

VILLAGE COMPUTERS
7 Great Jones St.
212-254-9191
Mon.-Sat.

Computer-phobes, take heart: The patient, expert salespeople here can make nearly any hardware or software seem user-friendly.

ENVIRONMENTALLY CONSCIOUS

FELISSIMO
10 W. 56th St.
212-247-5656
Mon.-Sat.

Four floors of a gorgeous Beaux-Arts townhouse dedicated to "environmentally conscious" home furnishings, fashion, linens, gardening accessories, and more; thanks to the Irish designer Clodagh, the place feels homier than most NY apartments. Don't miss the cozy upstairs tea room.

EYEWEAR

THE EYE MAN
2266 Broadway (81st-82nd. Sts.)
212-873-4114
7 days (closed Sun. July & August)

*You'll find all the top designer eyeglass frames
here, like Matsuda, Oliver Peoples, Armani, Modo,
L.A. Eyeworks, but the real advantage is extraordinary service; they also have a section just for
children, and replace broken frames free to age 12
— even if it's the kid's fault.*

UNIQUE EYEWEAR
19 W. 34th St.
212-947-4977
Mon.-Sat.
no c.c.

Joan & Gerry's Best Buy

*If you want exclusive or ultra-fancy, go elsewhere;
otherwise, you'll find unbelievable prices on a
huge choice of expertly fitted frames here. Before
you come, it's always a good idea to check your
prescription with an opthalmologist.*

FABRICS

ART MAX
250 W. 40th St.
212-398-0755
Mon.-Sat.

Joan & Gerry's Best Buy

Among garment district fabric stores, this one has the best selection and prices, plus polyglot sales-people who know their business.

CORA GINSBURG
19 E. 74th St.
212-744-1352
By appointment only

Antique textiles so beautiful it's hard to imagine touching them, never mind using them; museums, collectors, and designers often snatch up her finds immediately.

JOYCE'S JEMS
914-639-0659
By appointment only

Luxurious antique textiles, from heavy Victorian fabrics to woven brocades and velvets; there's also a wonderful collection of beaded and painted handbags.

KORDOL FABRICS
194 Orchard St.
212-254-8319
Sun.-Fri.

Fabric fanatics, take note; you can find some of the same high-quality cloths as Garment District stores for much less here.

PATERSON SILKS
36 E. 14th St.
212-929-7861
7 days

Joan & Gerry's Best Buy

Some consider this the city's best sewing supply store; knowledgeable salespeople, enormous selection give them a tight-knit case.

BECKENSTEIN MEN'S FABRICS
121 Orchard St.
212-475-6666
Sun.-Fri.

Joan & Gerry's Best Buy

Follow the city's top tailors to this secret source for men's suiting fabrics; you'll find fine-quality firsts and seconds.

FOOD
FOOD — Bakeries

A. ORWASHER BAKERY
308 E. 78th St.
212-288-6569
Mon.-Sat.

In business for 75 years, this place uses recipes even older for a huge variety of mouthwatering breads; don't miss the luscious raisin pumpernickel, or the sensual challah on Fridays.

A. ZITO AND SON'S BAKERY
259 Bleecker St.
212-929-6139
7 days

Fans line up at daybreak here for oven-fresh bread; once you taste the heavenly Italian, whole wheat, white, or Sicilian, you'll probably join them.

THE BREAD SHOP
3139 Broadway
212-666-4343
7 days
no c.c.

Beloved by Barnard and Columbia students, this "whole food" bakery turns out delicious breads, cakes, and cookies at wonderful prices; worth a visit if you're up here and hungry.

CAFE LALO
201 W. 83rd St.
212-469-6031
7 days

As close to Vienna as it gets in NYC, this bright, bubbling, boisterous Upper West Sider boasts some of the best cakes and pastries we've tasted; worth the inevitable wait for a table.

EROTIC BAKER
582 Amsterdam Ave.
212-362-7557
Tues.-Sat.

Along with notorious confections shaped like you-know-whats, this place has built a respectable business of late in artistic cakes the whole family can eat.

ECCE PANIS
1120 Third Ave.
212-535-2099
1620 Madison Ave.
212-348-0040
7 days

More than just food, bread becomes an artistic medium for these people; fantasies like chocolate bread and double walnut share the bill with scrumptious standards like whole-wheat currant and sourdough.

GERTELS
53 Hester St.
212-982-3250
Sun.-Fri.

Irresistible babkas, strudels, chocolate rolls, and cakes draw hordes, but the big attraction here is unparalleled potato kugel, made Thursdays only.

GROSSINGER'S UPTOWN
570 Columbus Ave.
212-874-6996
Sun.-Fri.

Columbus Avenue staple still serves up terrific cheesecakes and that famous praline ice cream cake; it's also the trendy Avenue's only remaining kosher shop.

H & H BAGEL
2239 Broadway (at 80th)
212-595-8000
7 days, 24 hours

The City's best bagels, some say, baked fresh from 2AM daily; that may also be the only hour you can buy them without eternal waits in line.

KOSSAR'S BIALYSTOCKER KUCHEN BAKERY
367 Grand St.
212-473-4810
7 days
No c.c.

Joan & Gerry's Best Buy

The most tantalizing bialys — flat, dense Jewish rolls — we've ever sampled; 24-hour bakery means they always come out fresh.

MOISHE'S HOMEMADE KOSHER BAKERY
181 E. Houston St.
212-475-9824

115 Second Ave.
212-505-8555
Sun.-Fri.
No c.c.

If you're a fan of hamentaschen — *the triangular, fruit-filled Jewish pastry — you owe yourself a trip to either branch of this old-fashioned bakery; like the rugelach, challah, cakes, and homemade bagels here, they're the real thing.*

NINTH ST. BAKERY
350 E. 9th St.
212-777-0667
7 days
No c.c.

Very East Village bakery with a tantalizing, inexpensive selection of Russian and peasant breads.

PATISSERIE LANCIANI
271 W. 4th St.
212-929-0739
7 days

Former Plaza pastry chef now creates luscious cakes, pastries, tortes, mousses, and breads in his own bakery/cafe; the food's more impressive than the surroundings.

RIGO HUNGARIAN
VIENNESE PASTRY
318 E. 78th St.
212-988-0052
Sun.-Tues.; closed Aug.

Gorgeous homemade European pastries that taste as wonderful as they look; the whole repertoire of strudels, tortes, petit fours, cakes, ana cookies is made without preservatives.

WHOLE EARTH BAKERY
70 Spring St.
212-226-8280

130 St. Mark's Pl.
212-677-7597
7 days
No c.c.

You'd never believe that the delicious muffins, scones, and breads from these family-owned bakeries are all-natural, organic, and even sweetened without sugar.

FOOD — Candy

THE CHOCOLATE GALLERY
34 W. 22nd St.
212-675-2253
Mon.-Sat.

Along with delicious chocolates by the pound, confectionary tools are the sweetest find here; they give classes on cake decorating, chocolate modeling, and marzipan-making, too.

CHOCOLATE PHOTOS
637 W. 27th St.
212-714-1880
Mail Order only

Love someone so much you want to eat them up? Now you can. Working from a photo, these people will imprint 250 chocolates with your sweetheart's visage; for a perfect wedding gift, they can print names of the couple-to-be. Corporate logos, too.

DAVID'S CANDIES
101-07 Jamaica Ave., Richmond Hill
Queens, NY
718-849-7750
Tues.-Sat.
No c.c.

They don't make them like they used to — except here, where every chocolate's still homemade and hand-dipped. Immense variety, friendly service.

ELK CANDY
240 E. 86th St.
212-650-1177
7 days
No c.c.

Marzipan is the specialty at this delightful, old-fashioned Upper East Side source; especially sweet for holiday candies.

EVELYN CHOCOLATES
4 John St.
212-267-5170
Mon.-Sat.

Charming chocolate sculptures distinguish this Financial District shop.

LEONIDAS
485 Madison Ave.
212-980-2608
7 days

Only US outpost of Belgium's most popular choco-
latier; pricy, to-die-for truffles, pralines, marzi-
pan.

LI-LAC CHOCOLATES
120 Christopher St.
212-242-7374
800-624-4874
7 days

A Village landmark for chocoholics for nearly 70
years; irresistible homemade chocolates, truffles,
and marzipan.

MONDEL HOMEMADE
CHOCOLATES
2913 Broadway
212-864-2111
7 days

Students and faculty from nearby Columbia have
long rhapsodized over Mondel's homemade choco-
lates; from anywhere, it's worth trekking up here
for unusual flavors and beautiful gift packages.

SCHWARTZ CHOCOLATE
31 Denton Ave.
New Hyde Park, NY 11040
800-522-2462
7 days

This place is famous for all its mouth-watering chocolates, but connoisseurs truly treasure the homemade chocolate-covered marshmallows (and a sinful version with caramel filling).

WOLSK'S CONFECTIONS
81 Ludlow St.
212-475-7946
Sun.-Fri.

Joan & Gerry's Best Buy

Just walking in brings on a sugar rush; hand-dipped chocolates, 50 varieties of fresh-roasted nuts, 30 kinds of dried fruits at old-fashioned prices.

FOOD — Cheese & Dairy

ALLEVA DAIRY
188 Grand St.
212-226-7990
7 days
No c.c.

In business a century, this place is America's oldest ricotta and mozzarella maker; these days, they also carry a complete line of Italian specialties.

BEN'S CHEESE SHOP
181 E. Houston St.
212-254-8290
Sun.-Fri.
No c.c.

Aficionados we know won't buy their cream cheese or farmer's cheese anywhere else; along with the classic, you'll find farmer's cheese flavors like nut-and-raisin, blueberry, strawberry, and pineapple.

DI PAL'S LATTICINI FRESCA
206 Grand St.
212-226-1033
7 days
no c.c.

Family-run dairy store still makes its own moz-zarella, ricotta, and fresh pasta; even first-timers get treated like long-lost relatives.

EAST VILLAGE CHEESE STORE
34 Third Ave.
212-477-2601
7 days
No c.c.

Joan & Gerry's Best Buy
From all over town, they trek to this neighborhood institution, and it's worth the trip; terrific prices on wonderful cheeses, cold cuts, pastas, and cof-fees.

IDEAL CHEESE SHOP
1205 Second Ave.
212-688-7579
Mon.-Sat.

Mecca for cheese lovers, with the nation's largest

*selection of goat and sheep cheese; they also claim
the most low-fat and low-cholesterol varieties.*

MURRAY'S CHEESE SHOP
257 Bleecker St.
212-243-3289
7 days
No c.c.

Joan & Gerry's Best Buy
*Neighborhood staple offers huge variety of import-
ed cheeses, 15 kinds of olives, and delicious fresh
pastas and breads at terrific prices; they actually
<u>invite</u> you to sample the goods here.*

FOOD — Coffee & Tea

DANAL
90 E. 10th St.
212-982-6930
Weds.-Sun.
No c.c.

*If L.L. Bean opened a tea parlor, it would look like
this; charming, cozy cafe serves scrumptious sandwiches, gift shop sells domestic and exotic teas.*

McNULTY'S
109 Christopher St.
212-242-5351

247 Columbus Ave.
212-362-4700
7 days

*More than 100 varieties of delicious coffees and
rare teas at great prices; ask about any blend they
stock, and you'll get a lively dissertation on its
merits.*

PORTO RICO
IMPORTING COMPANY
201 Bleecker St.
212-477-5421
Mon.-Sun.

*Canvas bags hanging off the wall offer delicious,
fresh-roasted coffee beans; few fancy flavors
among the 40 or so they stock, but the blends we've
sampled always taste perfect.*

SCHAPIRA'S
117 W. 10th St.
212-675-3733
7 days

*Old-fashioned West Village source for top-quality
coffee beans; friendly, knowledgeable proprietors
make picking blends a pleasure.*

FOOD — Deli

LUDLOW 85 CAFE
85 Ludlow St.
212-979-8585
Sun.-Fri.
No c.c.

*A rarity on the Lower East Side: A Kosher vege-
tarian restaurant with fresh salads as well as the
traditional blintzes-and-matzoh-brei fare.*

TODARO BROTHERS
555 Second Ave.
212-532-0633
7 days

*More than a deli, less than a supermarket, this
place is best for cheeses, Italian cold cuts, and
bread; friendly, chatty counter help.*

SCHACHT
90 Second Ave.
212-420-8219
7 days

*Less-expensive-than-most East Village source for
Nova, smoked fish, and bagels.*

FOOD — Health Foods

BROWNIE FOODS
91 Fifth Ave.
212-242-2199
Mon.-Sat.

*Ignore the dreary storefront; inside this health-
food supermarket, you'll find a seemingly endless
selection of breads, grains, vitamins, herbs, teas.*

COMMODITIES
117 Hudson St.
212-334-8330
7 days

More natural and organic foods than you ever knew existed, spread over 5,000 square feet of a Tribeca warehouse; enormous variety.

NATIVE FARMS ORGANIC
322 E. 11 St.
212-614-0727
7 days
No c.c.

Outside, it looks like a country general store; inside, there's a beautiful selection of organic produce and fresh breads.

WHOLE FOODS IN SOHO
117 Prince St.
212-673-5388
7 days

Mega-market for natural food features first-rate fresh fish department, pricy organic produce, terrific natural cosmetics and vitamins, more.

FOOD — Markets

BALDUCCI'S
424 Sixth Ave.
212-673-2600
7 days

Always-packed gourmet emporium keeps winning new fans with impeccable cheeses, coffees, fresh pastas, salads, and breads, smoked fish, meats; crowded aisles can make weekend shopping feel more like amateur wrestling.

DEAN & DELUCA
560 Broadway
212-431-1691
7 days

Soho style and attitude pervade this huge food boutique, with the best fish, coffees, cheeses, breads, prepared foods and imports at prices to match; for a real scene, visit their espresso bar around lunchtime.

FAIRWAY
2127 Broadway
212-595-1888
7 days
No c.c.

Joan & Gerry's Best Buy
Never mind the irresistible cheeses, pastas, breads, and fish here; weekends, it becomes the biggest people-watching scene north of the night-clubs.

FISHER & LEVY
875 Third Ave.
212-832-3880
Mon.-Fri.

All of the scrumptious prepared foods here — from breakfast items to gourmet pizzas to overstuffed sandwiches — can be delivered to home or office; crack catering operation also does a terrific job for big parties.

GOURMET GARAGE
47 Wooster St.
212-941-5850
7 days
no c.c.

Side by side with the city's top chefs, you can shop for exquisite gourmet foods here at wholesale prices here; gorgeous, exotic produce like wild mushrooms and baby vegetables, luscious cheeses, rich coffees, smoked fish, more. Come early; the selection gets limited.

GRACE'S MARKETPLACE
1237 Third Ave.
212-737-0600
7 days

Grace's offers the neighborhood's best selection of produce, cheeses, prepared foods, baked goods, and candy; tremendous selection.

RUSS & DAUGHTERS
179 E. Houston St.
212-475-4880
7 days

For first-class nuts, fruits, pate, smoked fish, and even well-priced caviar, trust this Lower East Side staple, family-owned for generations.

ZABAR'S
2245 Broadway
212-787-2000
7 days
Mezzanine open 9-6 daily

Joan & Gerry's Best Buy

For food, its icon status extends far beyond the city; but some out-of-towners miss the fabulous selection of well-priced kitchen equipment upstairs.

FOOD — Meats & Fish

BARNEY GREENGRASS
541 Amsterdam Ave.
212-724-4707
Sun.-Tues.

Closed on Passover and the first 3 weeks of Aug.

Self-proclaimed "sturgeon king" earns his crown with near-perfect smoked fish delicacies, as well as delicious cream cheeses and salads; don't miss Sunday brunch, an Upper West Side institution.

CAVIARTERIA
29 E. 60th St.
212-759-7410; 1-800-4-CAVIAR
Mon.-Sat.

Mostly mail-order operation also retails top-quality caviar, pates, and smoked salmon; wholesale business means some of the City's best prices.

CENTRAL FISH COMPANY
527 Ninth Ave.
212-279-2317
Mon.-Sat.
No c.c.

Brave the Hell's Kitchen location and you'll discover one of the City's most extensive selections of fresh fish at wholesale prices.

CITARELLA FISH & MEATS
2135 Broadway
212-874-0383 (fish)
212-874-0909 (meats)
7 days

Esteemed fish market has jazzed itself up with an upscale "meat boutique" and takeout business; the sauces, homemade sausage, and custardy rice pudding are wonderful.

JEFFERSON MARKET
455 Sixth Ave.
212-675-2277
7 days

For meat fresher than this, you'd have to go hunting; top-quality fish, poultry, produce, and salads, too.

KUROWYCKY MEATS
24 First Ave.
212-477-0344
Mon.-Sat.
No c.c.

*They never had it this good in the Old Country;
delicious meats, irresistible sausages, and mouth-
watering Eastern European breads and condi-
ments.*

M & A INTERNATIONAL FOOD
106 Baltic St.
Brooklyn, NY
718-797-3535
718-625-7465

*From mid-November until January 1, this whole-
saler opens its doors to give what the owner calls
"a taste of real caviar" at unbelievable prices;
smoked salmon and foie gras, too.*

NEVADA MEAT MARKET
2012 Broadway
212-362-0443
Mon.-Sat.
No c.c.

*At this Yupper West Side butcher, you'll find wild
game like duck, goose, and pheasant at slightly
above-average prices.*

RAOUL'S
179 Prince St.
212-674-0708
7 days

*A Parisian charcuterie transplanted to Soho; first-
class meats share the cases with sumptuous
sausages, near-perfect hams, terrines, and salads.*

REGENT FOODS
1174 Lexington Ave.
212-744-3450
Mon.-Sat.

Looks like a regular butcher shop, but you'll find unusual meats like quail, pheasant, and partridge here.

PREMIER VEAL
555 West St.
212-243-3170
Mon.-Fri.

Wholesale prices, no minimum make a trip worthwhile to this Meat District veal supplier; team up with friends and bulk orders will total a fraction of butcher-store prices.

FOOD — Pasta

BIANCA PASTA
22-24 Carmine St.
212-242-4961
Mon.-Sat.
no c.c.

Family-run pasta emporium also sells homemade sauces and fresh cheeses; for non-dairy eaters and vegetarians, there's also a scrumptious vegetable-only ravioli.

BRUNO RAVIOLI CO.
653 Ninth Ave.
212-246-8456
Mon.-Sat.

Joan & Gerry's Best Buy

In the family more than a century, this Hell's Kitchen stalwart has evolved into one of the City's top sources for creative, delicious fresh pastas, homemade sauces, and ready-to-heat dishes.

MORISI'S MACARONI COMPANY
647 5th Ave.
Brooklyn, NY
718-788-2299
Mon.-Sat.
No c.c.

Joan & Gerry's Best Buy

For purists who cringe at the thought of boxed pasta, this place has more than 200 fresh varieties in 50 flavors like cajun and blueberry.

PIEMONTE RAVIOLI CO.
190 Grand St.
212-226-0475

To sample their pasta, eat in a local trattoria (this place supplies many) or stop in here; you'll find a mind-boggling variety of pasta they make fresh every day.

RAFFETTO'S
144 W. Houston St.
212-777-1261
Tues.-Sat.
no c.c.

*Mamma herself would be proud of these fresh, tradition-
al pastas, a family specialty here for almost 90 years;
you can also get pasta sheets cut to your specifications.*

FOOD — Specialty Foods

GUSS PICKLES
35 Essex St.
212-254-4477
Sun.-Fri.
no c.c.

*Center of the universe for pickle lovers, with fresh-from-
the-barrel sours, half-sours, and a variations; new pick-
led celery and carrots add a `90s health twist.*

HORS D'OEUVRES UNLIMITED
4209 Dell Ave.
North Bergen, NJ 07047
800-648-3787
201-865-4545
Mon.-Fri.

*Entertaining, but don't want to pay a caterer?
Here's the next best thing. Scrumptious appetizers
and hors d'oeuvres flash-frozen and shipped ready
to heat or eat; vegetarian and kosher options, too.*

KALUATYAN'S
123 Lexington Ave.
212-685-3451
7 days

On a stretch of Lexington Ave. that has become Little Bombay, this place remains new York's oldest Indian store; terrific selection of imported foods.

KAM MAN FOOD PRODUCTS
200 Canal St.
212-571-0330
7 days

Joan & Gerry's Best Buy

Browsing here feels like a momentary trip across the globe; everything from fish, meat (they line up for the duck) to housewares to exotic Chinese remedies.

MYERS OF KESWICK
634 Hudson St.
212-691-4194
7 days

Love British food, but hate the trip to London? Check out this Lower West Side purveyor of all things English; kidney pie, Stilton, kippers, sausage, and imported British specialties you won't find anywhere else.

OLD DENMARK
133 E. 65th St.
212-744-2533
Mon.-Sat
No c.c.

*Fresh and clean, Scandinavian food has found a
following lately among New York foodies; you can
discover it all at this Midtown tearoom-market.*

PAPRIKAS WEISS IMPORTERS
1572 Second Ave.
212-288-6117
Mon.-Sat.

*Eye-popping variety of Middle Eastern foods,
unusual spices, candies, French pates, traditional
Hungarian foods, canned goods, even gift items.*

SANADI IMPORTING COMPANY
187 &189 Atlantic Ave.
Brooklyn, NY
718-624-5762
Mon.-Sat.
No c.c.

*Nearly a century old, this place still offers one of
the City's best selections of dried fruits, nuts, and
Middle Eastern specialties; when in Brooklyn,
take a detour here.*

FOOD — Spices

APHRODISIA
282 Bleecker St.
212-989-6440

More than 200 herbs and spices mingle to make walking in here an ethereal experience; from a selection of fragrant barks and woods, you can also blend your own potpourri.

HOT STUFF
227 Sullivan St.
212-254-6120
Wed.-Mon.

Want to hear a spicy story? This Soho newcomer stocks every kind of hot spice, sauce, and jelly, from plain tabasco to "Satan's Revenge."

PETE'S SPICE AND EVERYTHING NICE
174 First Ave.
212-254-8773
7 days

Joan & Gerry's Best Buy

For serious cooks and professional caterers, this is the source for bulk herbs, spices, coffees, teas, grains, nuts, and gourmet items at budget prices.

FIREPLACES

ARGOLD INTERNATIONAL
110 BiCounty Blvd. (suite 122)
Farmingdale, NY 11735
516-293-5779
Mon.-Fri; call for weekend hours

Joan & Gerry's Best Buy

Fireplace equipment manufacturer's warehouse features tool sets, baskets, enclosures at a discount.

WILLIAM H. JACKSON
210 E. 58th St.
212-753-9400
Mon.-Fri

If an older NYC apartment building has a working fireplace, chances are this 165-year-old company installed it; nowadays, their showroom offers hundreds of fireplace mantels, andirons, screens, and fire sets.

FLOWERS, PLANTS, & PLANTERS

CHRISTOFFER'S
860 Mountain Ave.
Mountainside, NJ 07092
908-233-0500
Mon.-Sat.

Spectacular flower baskets and dried arrangements for weddings, parties, special occasions.

CLAYCRAFT
807 Sixth Ave.
212-242-2903
Mon.-Sat.

Manhattan's only outdoor garden center carries planters, fiberglas display pieces, baskets, pottery, garden furniture, even trees at Christmas.

DIANA GOULD
832 Scarsdale Ave.
Scarsdale, NY 10583
914-725-3844
7 days
No c.c.

With fresh and wild flowers, Gould concocts breathtaking natural arrangements; she's done flowers for some major New York weddings. Unique gift baskets, too.

FARM AND GARDEN NURSERY
2 Sixth Ave.
212-431-3577
7 days; call for Jan. and Feb. hours

City mice can see what a real country nursery looks like here; fruit trees, grass seed, vegetable plants for urban farmers.

GRASS ROOTS GARDEN
131 Spring St.
212-226-2662
Tues.-Sat.

Plants exotic and domestic, from $25 potted vari-
eties to $150 curiosities; decorating service can
match plants to your environment.

HOBENSACK AND KELLER
PO Box 96; Bridge St.
New Hope, PA 18938
215-862-2406
7 days
No c.c.

Even museums shop here for antique garden
appointments and superb, well-priced reproduc-
tions, from benches to urns to fountains; you'll
also find a good selection of oriental rugs.

MARLO FLOWERS
428A E. 75th St.
212-628-2246
Mon.-Fri.

Weekends call for appointment

Imaginative, exquisite floral arrangements, with
prices to match; we've seen their spectacular
designs at some very tony weddings.

PATCHOGUE FLORAL'S
FANTASY LAND
10 Robinson Ave.
E. Patchogue, NY 11772
516-475-2059
Mon.-Sat.

One of the East Coast's largest silk flower outlets, they also create exquisite arrangements; wholesale fresh flowers and bridal accessories, too.

SUPERIOR FLORIST
828 Sixth Ave.
212-679-4065
Mon.-Sat.

They buy their flowers directly from the farm, so you avoid the florist/deli markup here; impeccable quality.

FUR

BONNIE MARINO
BIEN SHEARLING
345 Seventh Ave., 24th floor
212-967-4646
Mon.-Fri. by appointment
No c.c.

When you want shearlings, minks, or fur hats, call Bonnie, a shopper who's earned the moniker "the shearling lady"; everyone has sales, but she has styles you won't find anywhere else discounted up to 40% off retail.

FLEMINGTON FUR COMPANY
8 Spring St.
Flemington, NJ 08822
908-782-2212
7 days

Joan & Gerry's Best Buy
Hardly the world's glamour capitol, but Flemington has become the fur-lover's Mecca; excellent service and terrific prices on high-quality, luxurious furs. They've also got a "Town & Country" department with good deals on handsome leathers and suedes.

G. MICHAEL HENNESSY FURS
333 Seventh Ave.
212-695-7991
Mon.-Fri.; Sat. by appointment

Joan & Gerry's Best Buy
Top-of-the-line furs at rock-bottom prices, with the best deals on mink; Hennessy himself was a fur trader and former president of Maximillian furs.

H.B.A. FUR CORPORATION
150 W. 30th St
212-564-1080
Mon.-Fri.; Sat. (Oct-Jan)

Bob Mackie designs for them, so you probably won't find anything understated; if money is no object, this is the place for chic furs and shearlings.

LEVENSON FURS
375 7th Ave
Mon.-Sat.
(after Labor Day)

Recycling has hit the fur trade; this old-fashioned furrier can transform your old furs into lining for a wool coat or raincoat.

FURNITURE

FURNITURE — Beds & Bedding

ARISE FUTON MATTRESS COMPANY
415 Amsterdam Ave.
212-362-1863

652 Broadway
212-475-7722

1296 Third Ave.
212-988-7274

265 W. 72nd St.
212-496-8410
7 days

Where you buy a futon — the folding Japanese "mattress" — is as important as the kind you buy; Arise has become a trusted source for futons and accessories.

THE CHARLES P. ROGERS
BRASS BED COMPANY
899 First Ave.
1-800-272-7726
212-935-6900
7 days

A real legend, this company started in 1855, when brass beds were "the latest thing;" their artisans still build beds one at a time. Factory prices, so if you thought you couldn't afford one of these, call them.

DIAL-A-MATTRESS
31-10 48th Ave.
Long Island City, NY 11101
718-472-1200
800-M-A-T-T-R-E-S

The same day you phone in your mattress order, they'll deliver and assemble it (provided it's in stock); competitive prices, too. We swear by them.

ECONOMY FOAM CENTER
173 E. Houston St.
212-473-4462
7 days

Foam mattresses and cushions cut to size while you wait, plus a wide selection of futons cheaper than Uptown.

ELEGANT BRASS BEDS
1460 65th St.
Brooklyn, NY 11219
718-256-8988
Sun.-Thurs.

At this brass bed manufacturer, you can actually watch them make your bed; their engraved fittings from Europe add a classy decorative touch.

1-800 TRY A BED
1-800-879-2233

Joan & Gerry's Best Buy

A godsend for busy people. Free delivery and setup, usually the same day; 70% off retail on Sealy, Serta, Simmons, SpringAir mattresses, Somma Waterbeds.

FURNITURE — Children's

ALBEE'S
715 Amsterdam Ave.
212-662-5740
Mon.-Sat.

Infants and tots should take their parents shopping here; they'll find terrific baby furniture and accessories from Childcrest, Simmons, Aprica, Morigeau.

BABY'S BEST
908-946-2378
calls only; 24 hour answering machine
No c.c.

Joan & Gerry's Best Buy

Truly pampered kids don't pick furniture — their parents hire decorators like this to do it; through the service, you can also order furniture, wall hangings, and strollers up to 40% off retail.

THE CRIB OUTLET
163 A Route 22W
Union, NJ 07083
908-686-6733
7 days

Joan & Gerry's Best Buy

Worth the trip for Bassett, Simmons, Childcraft, Perego, and Aprica cribs discounted 15-30%.

HUSH-A-BYE
1459 First Ave.
212-988-4500
7 days

Very friendly, old-fashioned source for nursery and kiddie furniture, layette sets, personalized quilts; you'll even find toys, books, and videos.

LEWIS OF LONDON
175 Route 4 W.
Paramus, NJ 07652
201-843-8224
Mon.-Sat

Whimsical furniture and accessories to brighten up a kid's room; scaled-down cars, circuses, trains, castles, dollhouses, carousels, and even old-fashioned cribs.

MARTIN FURNITURE
601 Kennedy Blvd.
West NY, NJ
201-864-1234

ACE BEDDING
331 Bloomfield Ave.
Montclair, NJ
201-783-6440

Both of these sources sell those racing car beds kids love.

NORMAN'S
1714 So. Second St.
Philadelphia, PA 19148
215-334-0632
Mon.-Sat.

Joan & Gerry's Best Buy

Gigantic selection of kids' furniture, tot to teenage, from Childcraft cribs to Simmonds, Bassett, and Prego beds and accessories.

ROCK-A-BYE-BABY
4150 Merrick Road
Massapequa, Long Island 11758
516-799-2229
7 days

Joan & Gerry's Best Buy

Kiddie department store with strollers, high chairs, car seats, and bedding from names like Simmons and Aprica; fair prices, terrific service.

SCHNEIDER'S
20 Ave. A
212/228-3540
7 days

Joan & Gerry's Best Buy

Longtime neighborhood children's furniture source with warm service, good prices on Childcraft, Simmons, McClaren, Vermont Precision; in-house repairs.

STORYBOOK HEIRLOOMS
1215 O' Brien Dr.
Menlo Park, CA 94025
800-825-6565
(Phones are open Mon.-Sun. 9am-1am Eastern Standard Time)

Busy parents will find the best children's furniture, playthings, and accessories from around the world in this catalog; not cheap, but a wonderful resource.

FURNITURE — *General*

ADIRONDACK STORE
109 Saranac Ave.
Lake Placid, NY 12946
518-523-2646
7 days

Along with traditional wooden lawn chairs — a
specialty — you'll find white birch accessories,
hickory furniture, rustic knick-knacks; if you don't
feel like journeying Upstate, shop by mail.

AMISH FARMS
37 Union Square W.
212-924-3180
Mon.-Sat.

Joan & Gerry's Best Buy
Really a glorified deli, with produce, dried fruits,
and the like; the real reason to look here is the
simple, solid, handmade Amish furniture.

APARTMENT LIVING
(NORTH CAROLINA
FURNITURE SHOWROOMS)
12 W. 21st St.
212-260-5050/260-5850
7 days

Joan & Gerry's Best Buy
Browse at furniture stores, then come here to buy.

They've got top names like Lexington, Henredon, and Stanley for up to 65% off retail.

ARNE SMITH
7599 Saulsbury Rd.
Tully, NY 13159
315-696-5776
7 days

Smith custom-designs the rustic twig furniture sold at most of the tony upstate "country" stores; tables start at $700, cupboards at $1,200.

BARTON SHARPE
119 Spring St.
212-925-9562
7 days

So you want classic American 18th-early 19th century furniture? Either steal it from a museum or buy beautiful reproductions here; for a fraction of the originals, you'll also find gorgeous period flatware and tableware knockoffs.

BON MARCHE
55 W. 13th St.
212-620-5550
1060 Third Ave.
212-620-5592
7 days

Look here first for home or office furniture; downtown, you'll find discounted bookcases, dressers, tables, chairs on the 6th floor, and lighting, and *fabulous clearance items on 7 (we found a huge oak bookcase for about $115). For even bigger bargains, take the pieces home and assemble them yourself. Uptown offers a microcosmic version of the Village warehouse.*

CASTRO CONVERTIBLES SHOWROOM
1990 Jericho Turnpike
New Hyde Park, NY 11040
516-488-3000
800-CASTRO-8 (800-227-8768)
7 days

Don't underestimate Castro — they've entered the `90s with good-looking fabrics, terrific styles, and the most comfortable convertible sofas; watch for their fabulous 2 for 1 sales.

CONRAN'S
2-8 Astor Place   212-505-1515

160 E. 53rd St.
212-371-2225; 800/431-2718
7 days

Young, fresh, and clean-looking housewares and home-furnishings, including affordable knockoffs of expensive designs; great deals on bookcases. The stores are being revitalized by a former Bloomingdales executive, and look better than ever.

DEER CHASE ANTIQUES (REPRODUCTIONS)
P.O. Box 194
Morris Plains, NJ 07950
201-538-6186
7 days

Forget one-of-a-kind. For much less than the original, these people can copy any piece of antique furniture; such meticulous work, it's hard to tell theirs from the real thing.

ELLENBURG'S WICKER AND CASUAL
I-40 and Stamey Farm Rd.
PO Box 5628
Statesville, NC 28677
704-873-2900

Joan & Gerry's Best Buy

Through the mail, these people specialize in discounted wicker and rattan from names like Lloyd Flanders, Henry Link, and Lane.

E. POLAROLO AND SON
11 E. 12th St.
212-255-6260
Mon.-Sat.
No c.c.

Expert furniture restoration and reupholstering by a third-generation family business; for work this good, prices seem a bargain.

EXPRESSIONS CUSTOM FURNITURE
680 Stewart Ave.   516-222-6020
Westbury, NY
7 days

With more than 150 frame styles and 600 fabrics and leathers here, you should be able to design a sofa that suits you; beautiful work, but not cheap.

FOREMOST FURNITURE SHOWROOMS
8 W. 30th St.
212-889-6347
7 days

Joan & Gerry's Best Buy

Discounts on names like Henredon, Stanley, and Century make this place enough of a find. But spectacular floor sales — when everything goes for closeout prices — make it bargain heaven. You may want to bring roller skates; there's 48,000 feet of display space over four floors, including a full floor of leather creations.

THE FURNITURE CONNECTION
Holmdel, NJ
Phone calls only
908-946-2378

Joan & Gerry's Best Buy

High-end, traditional furniture discounted up to

50%; since they only deal by phone, you might want to compare through catalogs or showrooms first.

FURNITURE EXPO
1 Bruce Ave.
Stratford, CT 06497
203-575-6686
800-969-EXPO
7 days

Find the name and model # of the furniture or bedding you want; they'll get it, discounted 30-50%. Try them before you buy retail.

G&J VAN DAM
3414 Church Ave.
Brooklyn, NY 11203
718-469-7216
718-327-4907
718-327-4993 (24 hours)
Mon.-Sat., by appointment

For a basic kitchen table set, it's hard to beat the deals here; they also reupholster recliners (from $350) and sofa beds (from $665).

THE HIGH POINT CHAMBER
OF COMMERCE
PO Box 5025
High Point, NC 27262
919-889-8151

Joan & Gerry's Best Buy

Scour their brochure for High Point's famous furniture factories, then work the phones to see which will sell directly to you.   Before you order, you'll need the make and model number of a piece; you should also obtain the service and repair policies in writing.   Slightly-above-wholesale prices make the time and effort worth it.

IRREPLACEABLE ARTIFACTS
14 2nd Ave.
212-777-2900
7 days

Looks like an earthquake hit it, but this fascinating showroom's really an amalgam of furniture and garden accessories from every period and style; check out the stone roof garden.

KATZ AND SONS
146 Essex St.
212/673-2184
Sun-Fri
c.c. only on deposits

Joan & Gerry's Best Buy

Up to half off retail, you'll find furniture from big names like Henredon, Pennsylvania House, Emerson Leather, Stanley, Sealy, and Simmons;

*for even biggger bargains, sneak across the street
to their clearance center.*

NOSTALGIA OAK WAREHOUSE
1 Jake Brown Road
Old Bridge,NJ 08857
908-679-1700

2075 Jericho Turnpike
New Hyde Park, NY 11040
516-328-1711

353B Englishtown Road
Jamestown, NJ 08331
908-446-4333

1057 Route 46 E.
Clifton, NJ 07013
201-777-9112
Thurs.-Tues.

Joan & Gerry's Best Buy
*Huge selection of very solid reproduction oak bed-
room, dining room, kitchen sets, curios, rockers,
and hutches; fantastic prices.*

OAKSMITH AND JONES
1321 Second Ave.
212-535-1451
7 days

*Can anyone tell reproductions from real antiques?
Not here; their solid oak, mahogany, and pine
copies look as good as old, and cost much less.*

OUTLET FOR LEATHER
4014 Promenade Shops at Main St.
Voorhees, NJ 08043
609-751-9111
7 days

Joan & Gerry's Best Buy

Into leather? Furniture, that is? This place has terrific prices on contemporary leather pieces from around the world.

PALM CASUAL FURNITURE
4001 South US 1
Rockledge, FL 32955
407-631-0232
7 days

Factory prices on tables, chairs, chaise longues, recliners, gliders, love seats, and sofas; call for a brochure.

SECOND CHANCE
40 W. Main St.
Southhampton, NY 11968
516-283-2988

45 W. Main St.
Southhampton, NY 11968
516-283-2988
7 days

Joan & Gerry's Best Buy

The buyer here frequents the same factory as Ralph Lauren's wicker furniture people; You'll also find antique linens, jewelry, china, and glassware.

SALVAGE BARN
525 Hudson St.
212-929-5787
7 days

Joan & Gerry's Best Buy

Affordable used and antique furniture, including some pieces you'd actually want to own; selection changes from week to week.

SHABBY CHIC
93 Greene St.
212-274-9842
7 days

Miss Havisham's furniture, if she lived in a fabulous loft; oversized, overstuffed, comfy-looking pieces in cream and white, along with neo-Victorian sconces and candelabras.

SWAN CREEK ARCHITECTURAL CENTER
333 N. Main St.
Lambertville, NJ 08530
609-397-4884
800-927-3004
7 days

Worth the drive for architectural antiques and rustic-looking handcrafted outdoor furniture; they also custom-build gazebos, doors, and posts.

VALLEY FURNITURE
20 Stirling Rd.
Watchung, NJ 07060
908-756-7623
7 days

You can hardly tell their affordable furniture clones from the originals; solid copies of Williamsburgh, Newport, Sturbridge, and Mission-style pieces.

FURNITURE — *Office*

CASELLA BROTHERS
198 Market St.
Elmwood Park, NJ 07404
201-791-0757
Mon.-Sat.
No c.c.

Small family business specializes in office furniture from Hon and Tiffany at not-bad prices; they also engrave plaques, nameplates.

CROWN DISCOUNT OFFICE PRODUCTS
4773 Sunrise Highway
Bohemia, NY 11716
800-222-PENS (7367)
7 days
Joan & Gerry's Best Buy

Reliable source for office furniture, computer peripherals, copy machines, and supplies discounted up to 40% off retail.

OFFICE FURNITURE
HEAVEN
22 W. 19th St.
212-989-8600
Mon.-Fri.

Terrific values in used office furniture and gorgeous closeouts from Knoll, Helikon, Joyce, Oxford; look here before you buy new.

UFO USED FURNITURE OUTLET
259 North Henry St.
Brooklyn, NY 11222
718-389-1144
Mon.-Fri.

Joan & Gerry's Best Buy

Refurbished, good-as-new office furniture, deeply discounted; steel case files, $700 new, go for $400 here; vertical files, $345 new, $175 here.

FURNITURE — Rental

A.F.R. THE FURNITURE
RENTAL PEOPLE
71 Third Ave.
212-867-2800
Mon.-Sat.

One of the City's biggest selections of furniture to rent, either by the piece or in sets; rent for as long or as short as you need.

COST PLUS FURNITURE RENTAL
44 E. 32nd St.
212-686-1177
Sun.-Fri.

Joan & Gerry's Best Buy

About as cheap as it gets to rent office and residential furniture; you'll recognize the names.

GAMES & TOYS

BIG CITY KITE COMPANY
1201 Lexington Ave.
212-472-2623
Mon.-Fri.
Sun. (seasonally)

Connoisseurs turn David Klein's creations into mobiles and wallhangings; he still makes flying models too, like dazzling tissue-paper fighter kites and looping stunt kites. Repair service; new dart center for boards and parts.

THE CHESS SHOP
230 Thompson St.
212-475-9580
7 days

At this rather dingy storefront, you can buy chess supplies, but the real action is at the boards; play for $1.50/hour with a crowd of neighborhood regulars.

THE DOLLHOUSE FACTORY
157 Main St.
Lebanon, NJ 08833
908-236-6404
Tues.-Sat. (open 7 days a week from Dec.-
Christmas)

*Wonderland for kids, a treasure for adult collec-
tors, this factory showroom boasts dollhouses, furniture, accessories, "how-to" books, supplies, tools
— and, yes, dolls. Call or write for their delightful catalog.*

THE LAST WOUND UP
1595 Second Ave.
212-288-7585
7 days

*Need to unwind? This place has a huge variety of
windup toys, from hoop-jumping dogs to drum-
pounding monkeys.*

MARION & COMPANY
147 W. 26th St.
212-727-8900
Mon.-Fri.

*Games are serious business here; you'll find every
type of board game, card, poker chips, blackjack
and crap tables, and dice (they manufacture their
own). Marion's antique slot machines also make
wonderful decorative pieces.*

PENNY WHISTLE TOYS
132 Spring St.
212-925-2088

448 Columbus Ave.
212-873-9090

1283 Madison Ave. (91st St.)
212-369-3868
7 days

A giant, bubble-blowing teddy bear sets the exuberant tone the minute you walk in here; everything from $2.50 finger toys to jungle gyms in the thousands. The selection's much more creative than the big commercial toy stores.

THE RED BALLOON
409 Main St.
Ridgefield, CT 06877
203-438-8606
Tues.-Sat.

This place has fabulous kids' furniture and clothing on consignment, but the real story is their huge annual toy sale the weekend before Thanksgiving.

RED CABOOSE
16 W. 45th St.
212-575-0155
Mon.-Sat.

Miss your train? Find a replacement at this depot for model trains, miniature railroad equipment, vintage Lionel and American Flyer models, and remote-controlled cars and boats.

TENZING & PEMA
956 Madison Ave.
212/288-8780
7 days

Kids tired of stimulating gifts like Ninja Turtles?
Bring them to this intelligent "gift store for older
children"; rare items from Civil War artifacts to
50 million-year-old fossils to French Foreign
Legion caps share shelves with real telescopes,
cameras, and encyclopedias.

V. LORIA
178 Bowery
212-925-0300
Mon.-Sat.

If you want authenticity, buy your billiard set
from this 80-year-old family business; fabulous
selection of gaming equipment, bowling items, too.

GENERAL MERCHANDISE

NATIONAL WHOLESALE LIQUIDATORS
632 Broadway
212-979-2400
7 days

Joan & Gerry's Best Buy

Every possible household, personal hygiene, and
even food item imaginable discounted on two
packed floors; it's become Downtown's trendiest
scene since the clubs.

GIFT BASKETS

BASKETFULL
1133 Broadway
800-645-GIFT
212-255-6800
7 days

Champagne Wishes, Indulgence, The Movies, Total Man — just a few of the clever, creative gift baskets from this mail-order-only source; call for their lovely catalog.

THE GIFTED ONES
200 Waverly Pl.
212-627-4050
Mon.-Fri.

Instead of picnic lunches, baskets now carry messages like Happy Birthday and Get Well Soon, and this place has some of the most imaginative. Inside their delightful apple-shaped Big Apple basket: Soho soda, NY-style cheesecake, "instant" Statue of Liberty capsules, miniature landmarks.

SANDLER'S
212-245-3112; 1-800-75-FRUIT
7 days

Along with sinful candies and chocolate chip cookies, these people specialize in beautifully presented gift and fruit baskets.

GIFTWARE, GLASS, & TABLEWARE

BLOCK CHINA WAREHOUSE STORE
14 Leonard St.
212-966-2839
Wed.-Sun.

Joan & Gerry's Best Buy

Shop this manufacturer's secret outlet for classy china, crystal, and giftware up to 70% off retail; you'll find the same goods you've seen in expensive specialty stores.

CERAMICA
59 Thompson St.
212-941-1307
Tues.-Sun.

Unusual Italian glass and ceramic pieces, from plates and bowls to ashtrays and glasses; you might think prices are in Lira, though.

CERAMICA GIFT GALLERY
1009 Sixth Ave.
212-354-9216
Mon.-Fri.

One more reason not to pay department-store prices for giftware; deep discounts on big-name brands of china, crystal, tableware, sterling flatware.

CAROLE STUPELL
29 E. 22nd St.
212-260-3100
Mon.-Sat.

Some of the City's best-dressed tables wear ultra-tasteful china, glassware, silver, tableware from here; no bargains, high quality.

D.F. SANDERS
952 Madison Ave.
212-879-6161
7 days

High-design gifts for home or office; Madison Ave. prices mean you may find certain items elsewhere for less. Check out subtle, stylish vases, flatware, and linens.

EASTSIDE GIFTS AND DINNERWARE
351 Grand St.
212-982-7200
Sun.-Fri.

Joan & Gerry's Best Buy
With high-class names like Limoges, Mikasa, and Oneida, this is one of the Lower East Side's best sources for discount tableware.

FISH'S EDDY
889 Broadway
212-420-9020

551 Hudson St.
212-627-3956
7 days

Joan & Gerry's Best Buy

Eclectic restaurant china remnants sold by the piece or the set at flea-market prices; heaven for browsers and knick-knack lovers.

GOLDMAN'S GIFT SHOP
315 Grand St.
212-226-1423
Sun.-Thur.

Joan & Gerry's Best Buy

A beloved old-fashioned Lower East Side bargain source; discounts on giftware names you won't believe, like Baccarat crystal and Lladro figurines.

JAMAR
1714 Sheepshead Bay Rd.
Brooklyn, N.Y. 11235
718-615-2222
Mon.-Sat.
Closed Mon. summer

Joan & Gerry's Best Buy

A secret source for famous-name silver, china, crystal, stainless, flatware, and ceramics; the owners claim they can beat any advertised price. Worth the trip; they take telephone orders, too.

JOMPOLE COMPANY
330 Seventh Ave.
212-594-0440
Mon.-Fri.
Call for Sat. hours
No c.c.

Joan & Gerry's Best Buy

Along with corporate gifts and premiums, Jompole stocks giftware names like Hummel, Lladro, and Norman Rockwell at deep discounts; watches and diamonds, too. They'll even special-order items they don't carry.

L.S. COLLECTION
765 Madison Ave.
212-472-3355
Mon.-Sat.

Tries so hard to feel like a museum, we're surprised they haven't started guided tours; high-end, high-priced dishes, vases, glassware, desk items, and leather goods.

LANAC SALES
73 Canal St.
212-925-6422
Sun.-Fri.

Joan & Gerry's Best Buy

On the fringe of the Lower East Side, you'll find this source for discount china, crystal, and flatware. P.S.: "Lanac" is Canal spelled backwards!

MICHAEL C. FINA
580 Fifth Ave.
212-869-5050
718 937 8484
Mon.-Sat

From around the world, smart shoppers phone here to order bridal gifts, china, crystal, silver, jewelry, sterling, flatware, and frames; you can visit, too. Sometimes Bloomingdale's can come in cheaper, so do your homework.

MIKASA OUTLET
25 Enterprises Ave.
Secacus, NJ 07090
201-867-6805
second store

LIFESTYLE
155 Sinvalco Rd.
Secaucus, NJ
210-398-0600

Joan & Gerry's Best Buy
The same tableware you've eyed in department stores, at prices you won't believe; the second store offers deals on more contemporary Mikasa goods.

ROGERS AND ROSENTHAL
22 W. 48th St. (room 1102)
212-827-0115
Mon.-Fri.
no c.c.

Secret source for china, silver, and crystal discounts every major brand up to 50% off retail; phone and mail orders only.

WOODEN INDIAN
60 W. 15th St.
212-243-8590
Tues.-Sat.
No c.c.

Quirky glassware emporium offers a surplus of the kitschy and cutesy, along with more basic pieces and serviceable china.

WOLFMAN-GOLD & GOOD COMPANY
116 Greene St.
212-410-7000
Mon.-Sat.

Genteel Soho outpost for countrified tableware, linens, kitchen, bathroom, and home accessories is a perfect pitstop for gift shopping; some great buys, like charming picture frames at 3 for $30 on a recent visit, but visit the cash machine before coming.

THE YELLOW DOOR
1308 Avenue M
Brooklyn, NY 11230
718-998-7382

Joan & Gerry's Best Buy
You'll think you're on Madison Avenue with high-class giftware, tableware, jewelry from top names like Lalique, Baccarat, Alessi, Villeroy & Boch; but since you're in Brooklyn, you save 20-30% off retail. Worth the trip.

HARDWARE

ANTIQUE HARDWARE STORE
9730 Eastern Road
Route 611
Kintnerville, PA 18930
715-847-2447; call for free catalog
Mon.-Sun.

Check out their catalog for vintage and reproduction Victorian plumbing fixtures like pedestal sinks, clawfoot tubs, faucets, cabinet hardware.

EIGEN PLUMBING SUPPLY
236 W. 17th St.
212-255-1200
Mon.-Fri.

Plumbing professionals get supplies here, as do smart shoppers; they find American Standard's complete line, as well as Elkay and Rund-Rheen.

GEORGE TAYLOR
SPECIALTIES COMPANY
100 Hudson St.
212-226-5369
Mon.-Fri.

Call this invaluable Tribeca source for obsolete plumbing replacement parts; if they don't have what you need, they can manufacture a comparable part in their machine shop.

KOLSON
653 Middle Neck Rd.
Great Neck, NY 11023
516-487-1224
Mon.-Sat.
No c.c.

Classy bathroom accessories and fixtures; they import their own shower baskets and shower heads, and carry big-name hardware.

KRAFT HARDWARE
306 E. 61st St.
212-838-2214
Mon.-Fri.

Original, very pretty Victorian bathroom fixtures, along with plumbing hardware, shower enclosures; impressive choice of sinks in marble, porcelain, or onyx.

LEE SAM PLUMBING AND HEATING SUPPLY
124 Seventh Ave.
212-243-6482
Mon.-Sat.

You could build an entire kitchen or bathroom with supplies from here; everything except floors and lights, including cabinets, faucets, and fixtures from brand names like American Standard, Kohler, Delta, Grohe, Robern, Blanco, Franke, Broadway, more.

LEGS, LEGS, LEGS
155 E. 52nd St.
212-755-2168
Mon.-Sat.

Hardware, hardware, hardware for bathroom and kitchen; classy decorator doorknobs, hinges, vanities, tabletops, cabinets — and legs for tables, chairs, more.

P.E. GUERIN
23 Jane Street
212-243-5270
7 days by appt. only; closed first two weeks of July

America's oldest decorative hardware firm crafts exquisite fixtures in brass, bronze, and more; their foundry — now in Valencia, Spain — can also copy or reproduce almost anything in those materials.

RENOVATOR'S SUPPLY
Cinema Plaza, Routes 202 and 31
Flemington, N.J. 08822
908-788-5340
7 days

Dickens at The Home Depot; Victorian-era decorative hardware like tin ceilings, cabinet knobs, hinges, and accessories for clawfoot tubs, pedestal sinks. They claim they can track down any type of plumbing or lighting fixture; professionals rave about this source.

SIMON'S HARDWARE
421 Third Ave.
212-532-9220
Mon.-Sat.

Neighbors trust this shop for everyday hardware as well as custom-made decorative fixtures.

HATS

HATS — General

ARNOLD HATTERS
620 8th Ave.
212-768-3781
7 days

Trendies, take note: this is the place for those hot Kangol caps, along with Stetson and Dobbs models. Check out their private-label, Australian outback-style hats, too.

BURANELLI HATS
101 Delancey St.
212-473-1343
7 days

Joan & Gerry's Best Buy

Beautiful imported hats from Italy and Ireland, as well as top names like Borsalino and Stetson; Lower East Side prices.

MODERN HATTERS
313 Third St.
Jersey City, N.J. 07302
201-659-1113
7 days
No c.c.

Joan & Gerry's Best Buy

Dickens might have depicted the old factory that houses this place; inside, you'll find Stetson, Borsalino, Adolfo, Mr. John, and Sylvia hats at up to 50% off retail.

VAN DYCK HATTERS
94 Greenwich Ave.
212-929-5696
Mon.-Sat.
No c.c.

Hat heaven; not only do they sell their own brand, Stetsons, and Borsalinos, but they'll clean, block, restyle, reband, or rejuvenate hats — dying arts all.

VESTURE
141 Atlantic Ave.
Brooklyn, NY
718-237-4126
Mon.-Sat.

Gorgeous high-design hats and hatboxes for much less than what you'd pay in Manhattan; worth the trip.

HATS — Men

JJ HAT CENTER
1276 Broadway
212-502-5012

Joan & Gerry's Best Buy

Probably the City's largest selection of Stetsons, along with a huge variety of men's hats from baseball caps to berets to bowlers.

WORTH & WORTH
331 Madison Ave.
212-867-6058
Mon.-Sat.

A gentleman's-gentleman hat source; fur, felt, and straw fedoras, cowboy hats, rain hats, and caps. They now carry ties as well.

HATS — Women

CARLOS NEW YORK HATS
45 W. 38th St.
212-869-2207
Mon.-Fri.

Joan & Gerry's Best Buy

A microscopic millinery where designer Carlos Lewis makes and displays high-style hats and custom chapeaux. Lewis must have his thinking cap working; senior citizens get a 5% discount here.

LOLA MILLINERY
2 E. 17th St.
212-366-5708
Wed.-Sun.

Lola Ehrlich's little shop would look at home on the Seine as it does in the Flatiron district; so would her dazzling hats. No bargains, but beautiful bonnets from classic to clever.

MISS VICKI'S MILLINERY AND GIFT SHOP
430 Anderson Ave.
Cliffside Park, NJ 07010
201-945-1023
Mon.-Sat.
No c.c.

Joan & Gerry's Best Buy
Antique furniture, frames, vintage jewelry on one charming side; dazzling custom-made hats on the other. Vintage hats from $5, too.

HOBBY & CRAFT

A. FEIBUSCH — ZIPPERS AND THREADS
30 Allen St.
212-226-3964
Sun.-Fri.
no c.c.

For repairs or accessorizing, this one-of-a-kind source carries every size, color, or style zipper, with matching thread; what they don't carry, they'll custom-create.

AMERICA'S HOBBY CENTER
146 W. 22nd St.
212-675-8922
Mon.-Sat.

Beautiful boats and planes — most under two feet. Marshall Winston's model emporium also sells miniature trains, cars, and helicopters, as well as supplies.

CREATIVE YARNS AND CRAFTS
1011 Sixth Ave.
212-719-5648
Mon.-Sat. (closed Sat. in summer)

Joan & Gerry's Best Buy

Every kind of sewing supply, discounted; terrific selection of hard-to-find basic wools, needlework thread, coned yarns, and needlepoint accessories.

SCHOOL PRODUCTS COMPANY
1201 Broadway (third floor)
212-719-5648
Mon.-Sat. (closed Sat. in summer)

Joan & Gerry's Best Buy

Weavers' wonderland, with huge range of looms, knitting machines, and supplies; crafts enthusiasts will appreciate the bookbinding material and marbling supplies for paper and cloth.

JEWELRY

THE BEAD STORE
1065 Lexington Ave.
212-628-4383

132 Spring St.
212-941-6450
7 days

The City's most complete source for beads offers a massive selection from around the world; ambitious do-it-yourselfers can take stringing lessons here.

CARLOS COLONNA
400 Madison Ave.
212-838-7980
Mon.-Fri.
(Sat. Thanksgiving-Christmas)

Need a master engraver to regale the family silver with your coat of arms? Colonna says that's his specialty; for more mundane tasks, like custom-designed jewelry, he also does exquisite work.

CHATHAM JEWELERS
94 Main St.
Chatham, NJ
201-635-9100
Tues.-Sat.

They specialize in beautiful custom pieces, but you'll also find a fabulous selection of new and antique jewelry here.

DESIGNS BY MAURICE JEWELRY OUTLET
31-00 47th Ave.
Long Island City, NY 11101
718-392-0404
Mon.-Fri.

All that glitters in this factory outlet costs much less than retail; 14-K, 18K, and faux pieces from $5 to $500,000.

EMPIRE DIAMOND AND
GOLD JEWELRY
Empire State Building, 66th floor
212-564-4777
Mon.-Sat.
No c.c.

Joan & Gerry's Best Buy

Check here before you buy diamonds anywhere else; they sell Gemological Institute of America-certified rocks for less than wholesale. They've also got great finds in estate jewelry and silver.

GAUNTLET
144 Fifth Ave., 2nd floor
212-229-0180
mail order: 415-592-9715
Tues-Sat

Body piercing's more popular than ever, but it's important to find someone reliable to do a safe, clean job; these people are the City's best-known piercers, and they also sell fine jewelry for more body parts than you can imagine.

KENNETH JAY LANE
725 Fifth Ave.
212-751-6166
Mon.-Sat.

Stunning copies of Tiffany, Cartier, and Van Cleef & Arpels almost outdo the real things; Lane's most famous piece — Barbara Bush's triple-strand pearls — still retails for less than $100.

MARKELL JEWELERS
100 Woodbridge Mall
Woodbridge, NJ
908-855-1600
7 days

*In a rush for special-occasion jewelry? This place
can cut out almost any shape in 14K gold while
you wait.*

MYRON TOBACK
25 W. 47th St.
212-398-8300
Mon.-Fri.; closed first two weeks in
July and Dec. 25-Jan. 1

Joan & Gerry's Best Buy

*Can't find that perfect bangle? Make it yourself.
Toback sells plate, wire, and tools, and oversees a
wholesale arcade where gold, gold-filled, and silver chain sell by the foot; inexpensive selection of
earrings and beads, too.*

OCINO
66 John St.
212-269-3636
Mon.-Fri.

*Most Wall St.-area jewelers stock schlocky gold
chains, but this one specializes in custom work
and redesigning; they also sell brand-name watches and gold by weight.*

RENNIE ELLEN
15 W. 47th St. (room 401)
212-869-5525
Mon.-Fri. by appt. only

Diamond district's first woman dealer offers some of 47th St.'s best buys on spectacular diamonds; we trust her.

SAITY JEWELRY
Trump Tower
725 Fifth Ave.
212-308-6570
Mon.-Sat.

Real masterpieces by Zuni, Navajo, Hopi, other Native American artisans in sterling silver, turquoise, coral, jet, mother-of-pearl.

SANKO CULTURED PEARLS
45 W. 47th St.
212-819-0585
Mon.-Fri.
No c.c.

Joan & Gerry's Best Buy

Cultured pearls at basic prices; the owner told us he plans to retire "in a year or two," so hurry in soon.

KITCHEN & BATHROOM ACCESSORIES

COUNTRY FLOORS
15 E. 16th St.
212-627-8300
Mon.-Sat.

Gorgeous tiles for kitchen, bathroom, and walls; high-quality with prices to match.

HASTINGS TILE
230 Park Ave. South
212-674-9700
Mon.-Sat.

Every color and pattern tile imaginable for the bathroom and kitchen; take a look at the exquisite Panelli collection of hand-painted ceramics.

HOWARD KAPLAN BATH SHOP
47 E. 12th St.
212-674-1000
Mon.-Fri.

Fabulous, functional bathroom antiques, from soap dishes and sinks to faucets and taps, and some of the most unusual bathtubs you've ever seen.

PRO KITCHEN WARE
204 Bowery
212-941-8118
Mon.-Sat.

Joan & Gerry's Best Buy

For cooks, heaven must look like this; seemingly boundless stocks of basic kitchenware, commerical kitchen supplies and accessories at fabulous prices.

SEPCO INDUSTRIES
491 Wortman Ave.   718-257-2800
Brooklyn, NY 11208
Mon.-Fri.

Joan & Gerry's Best Buy

Their 80-page catalog contains more bathroom fixtures than a plumbers' convention; smart designs, prices up to half off retail.

SIG GREENBAUM
38 Davey St.
Bloomfield, N.J. 07003
Mon.-Fri.

For some loft dwellers, chunky industrial kitchen equipment has become de rigueur; you'll find it here.

THE QUARRY
192 E. 32nd St.   212-679-2559
Mon.-Sat.

True do-it-yourselfers will find paradise here; there's a fabulous selection of gorgeous imported tiles, wallpaper, and bathroom and kitchen accessories.

WILLIAMS-SONOMA OUTLET
231 Tenth Ave.   212-206-8118
7 days

Joan & Gerry's Best Buy

Overstocks from Williams-Sonoma, Pottery Barn and Hold Everything stores; unbelievable deals on constantly changing choice of first-class housewares.

LEATHER

ANANIAS
197 Bleecker   212-254-9540

second store
A&S Plaza Mall
33rd and Sixth Ave   212-947-4814
7 days

Ananias' German and Chinese owners make all their handmade leathergoods in Greece. Both stores offer huge selections of purses, sandals, belts, wallets.

ARIVEL FASHIONS
150 Orchard St.   212-673-8992
7 days

Worth stopping in here only because Andrew Marc leather jackets occasionally surface.

AVIREX FACTORY OUTLET
33-00 47th Ave.   718-482-1997
Long Island City, NY
Tues.-Sat.

Joan & Gerry's Best Buy

Their trendy, WWII-inspired bomber jackets cover some of the best-dressed backs in town; here, they sell for as much as 75% off retail. You'll also find their sheepskin jackets, outerwear, and sportswear at deep discounts.

BRIDGE MERCHANDISE
98 Orchard St.
212-674-6320
Sun.-Thurs.; hours vary

If labels don't matter, come here for leather jackets that could pass for department-store goods; alterations available.

SUPERIOR REPAIR CENTER
133 Lexington Ave   212-564-2267

138 W. 72nd St.   212-769-2099
Mon.-Fri.
(open Sat. from Sept.-June)

One of the country's most trusted leather restoration houses also sells a terrific selection of name-brand handbags and luggage; "we repair everything but broken hearts," they claim, and they'd probably fix those perfectly.

LIGHTING

ARTEMIDE OUTLET
1980 New Highway
Farmingdale, L.I. 11735
516-694-9292
Mon.-Fri.

Joan & Gerry's Best Buy
A terrific source for bargain lamps that look

expensive, including Tizio; they sell overstocks and discontinued models for up to 75% off retail.

CITY KNICKERBOCKER
781 8th Ave
212-586-3939
Mon.-Fri.

This lamp hospital handles everything from rewiring, refinishing and remounting to refurbishing Tiffany lamps; real brass, not brass-plated, parts.

GRAND BRASS
221 Grand St.
212-226-2567
Tues.-Sat.
no c.c.

Much more than just brass, this is one of the city's best sources for lamp replacement parts, from chandelier crystals to glass globes.

JUST BULBS
938 Broadway (at 22nd St.)
212-228-7820
Mon.-Fri.

Cows. Lobsters. Laundry on a string. Along with these loony lightbulbs, you'll find 25,000 different types from "flame" to 58 varieties of white and fluorescent.

JUST SHADES
21 Spring St.
212-966-2757
Thurs.-Tues.

You guessed it — every kind of lampshade imaginable, to fit any fixture, for any budget.

KING'S CHANDELIER CO.
P.O. Box 667
Eden, NC 27288
919-623-6188; call for catalog.
Mon.-Sat.

Joan & Gerry's Best Buy

Manufacturer's prices on exquisite lighting fixtures, with spectacular crystal and polished brass collections.

LAMPS AND SHADES UNLIMITED
44 Elm St.
New Canaan, CT
203-966-1314
Mon.-Sat.

A favorite designers' source for handsewn and custom lampshades; exquisite work they can personalize with themes and colors you choose. Best buy: Brass standing lamps for under $100.

LOUIS MATTIA
980 Second Ave.
212-753-2176
Mon.-Fri.
No c.c.

You can have a lamp made here, or buy a refurbished model for much less than retail; you can also trust them for reliable repairs, rewiring, and cleaning of chandeliers and lamps.

MARVIN ALEXANDER
315 E. 62nd St.
212-838-2320
Mon.-Fri

Distinctive antique lighting fixtures, chandeliers, and sconces; in this neighborhood, don't expect bargains.

NEW YORK GAS
LIGHTING CO.
145-149 Bowery
212-226-2840
7 days

Traditional lamps, ceiling fans, and lighting fixtures at deep discounts; they've also started stocking end and coffee tables.

ROY ELECTRIC
1054 Coney Island Ave.
Brooklyn, NY 11230
718-434-7002
800-366-3340
Mon.-Sat.

Joan & Gerry's Best Buy

Fabulous designer source for bathroom lighting fixtures, in styles from Victorian to Art Deco to contemporary.

SMART SHADES CO.
127-03 20th Ave.
College Point, NY 11356
718-358-8454
7 days

Joan & Gerry's Best Buy

One of the last Tiffany stained glass manufacturers is also a factory source for lamps and shades they can customize at no extra charge; ceiling fans, too.

LUGGAGE

BETTINGER'S LUGGAGE SHOP
80 Rivington St
212-475-1690
212-674-9411
Sun.-Fri.

Joan & Gerry's Best Buy

Since 1914, this place has crafted beautiful custom luggage, and retailed every major brand; a real find.

ECLECTIQUES
483 Broome St.
212-966-0650
Tues.-Sun.

Lost your luggage? Find a fabulous replacement among the distinctive antique trunks, bags, and steamers here.

JOBSON'S LUGGAGE
666 Lexington Ave.
212-355-6846
800-221-5238 (out of NY state)
Mon.-Sat.

Midtown's full of luggage tourist traps, so it's a relief to find a reliable retailer; professional staff, big discounts, and in-house repairs make them stand out.

LEDERER
613 Madison Ave.
212-355-5515
Mon.-Sat.

From the location, you'd guess everything here costs a fortune, but reasonable prices on gorgeous handbags, briefcases, and luggage can surprise you.

LEXINGTON LUGGAGE
793 Lexington Ave.
212-223-0698
800-822-0404 (outside New York)

Joan & Gerry's Best Buy

Trustworthy neighborhood fixture carries major brands of luggage, briefcases, children's trunks, school bags, and wallets at excellent prices; ask for Elliot.

LUGGAGE PLUS
83 Orchard St.
212-966-9744
Sun.-Fri.

Joan & Gerry's Best Buy

Up to 40% off retail here, you'll find big names in luggage like Samsonite, Lark, American Tourister, Lucas, and Totes.

MAGIC

FLOSSO-HORNMANN MAGIC CO.
45 W. 34th St., Rm. 607
212-279-6079
Mon.-Sat.

Founded in 1865, America's oldest magic shop still has hundreds of tricks up its sleeve; they'll demonstrate them on request.

TANNEN'S MAGIC
6 W. 32nd St.
212-239-8383
Mon.-Sat.

With more than 5,000 tricks for sale and frequent magic shows, Tannen — the world's largest magic store — enchants pros and amateurs alike.

MAPS

HAGSTROM MAP AND TRAVEL CENTER
57 W. 43rd St.
212-398-1222
Mon.-Fri.

World-famous cartographers operate this fascinating Midtown shop; globes, books, atlases, nautical/aeronautical charts, and maps of all 50 states.

NESTER'S MAPS AND GUIDES
36 W. 36th St.
212-695-6031
Mon.-Fri.
No c.c.

*Can't locate a certain map? This place probably
carries it, along with guidebooks like the hard-to-
track-down Taxi Driver's Guide to New York.*

MEMORABILIA

FILAMENTS/ANIMATION
34 W. 13th St.
212-924-3576
7 days

*Beloved cartoon characters appear on all the toys
and accessories here; you may start browsing for
the kids, but you'll end up keeping everything for
yourself.*

LOST CITY ARTS
275 Lafayette St.
212-94108025
Mon.-Sat.

*Like a museum of American culture, but every-
thing's for sale, decorative, and quite fabulous;
nouveau "antiques" from mock movie marquees to
commercial signs to dolls share the cavernous
space.*

LITTLE RICKIE
49 1/2 First Ave.
212-505-6467
7 Days

Loony East Village shop with collectible kitsch like Elvis lamps, rubber chickens, lava lamps, kit-kat clocks; "Where Pee-Wee shops for Miss Yvonne."

MOVIE STAR NEWS
134 W. 18th St.
212-620-8160
Mon.-Sat.

Forget Planet Hollywood; you'll find the stars here, from Valentino to Tom Cruise to Madonna. Posters, books, photos, and cinema publicity for aficionados.

NOSTALGIA...AND
ALL THAT JAZZ
217 Thompson St.
212-420-1940
7 days
no c.c.

Still use slang like "cool" and "cats"?" You'll really dig the early radio programs, jazz recordings, soundtracks, and photo stills here.

THE POP SHOP
292 Layfayette St.
212-219-2784
Tues-Sat.

Like pilgrims to Mecca, fans of the late artist Keith Haring flock here for t-shirts, jackets, and posters; his hip-hop designs decorate the floors and walls, too.

MUSIC BOXES

RITA FORD MUSIC BOXES
19 E. 65th St.
212-535-6717
Mon.-Sat.

This only-in-New-York treasure carries everything from simple, inexpensive music boxes to dazzling five-figure rarities; there's also a fabulous selection of classic music boxes for kids.

MUSIC & MUSICAL INSTRUMENTS —

Musical Instruments

ARDSLEY MUSICAL INSTRUMENT SERVICE
212 Sprain Rd.
Scarsdale, NY 10583
914-693-6639
Mon.-Sat.

Instead of paying a fortune for new instruments, journey here for affordable drums, violins, and clarinets, new and secondhand.

CARMINE ST. GUITAR SHOP
42 Carmine St.
212-691-8400
Mon.-Sat.

Aspiring amateurs and professional pickers alike come here for electric and acoustic guitars; along with new and used instruments, these people also custom-build their own.

LAPIANA PIANO SALES
211 W. 20th St.
212-243-5762
7 days

Joan & Gerry's Best Buy

For any budget, this is the city's best source for pianos. New Kawai and Young Chang, used Steinways, Baldwins, Knabes; rebuilding and refinishing, too.

MANNY'S
156 W. 48th St.
212-819-0576
Mon.-Sat.

Fantastic electronic instruments at realistic prices; old-fashioned acoustic instruments, too. Many professional players on staff.

PRO PIANO
85 Jane St.
212-206-8794
Mon.-Sat.

Hamburg, Steinway, and Yamaha pianos at very fair prices; they rent, too.

MUSIC & MUSICAL INSTRUMENTS — *Sheet Music*

BINZER MUSIC HOUSE
218 E. 81st St.
212-737-1146
Mon.-Sat.
No c.c.

You'll find what must qualify as one of the world's most extensive sheet music inventories here; deals on guitars and small instruments, too.

THE JOSEPH PATELSON MUSIC HOUSE
160 W. 56th St.
212-582-5840
212-582-7350
Mon.-Sat.

Name that tune and you'll find the sheet music for it here; from baroque to Broadway to the Beatles, there's an immense and well-priced inventory.

NOVELTIES

JIMSON'S
28 E. 18th St.
212-477-3386
Mon.-Sat.

Let your inner child get silly with the gags and tricks from this novelty megastore.

RUBIE'S COSTUME COMPANY
One Rubie Plaza (120th St.)
Richmond Hill, NY 11418
718-846-1008
Mon.-Fri.
extended hours closer to Halloween

Joan & Gerry's Best Buy
All the costumes you see in toy and novelty stores come from here, America's largest costume manufacturer; worth a visit for big discounts and selection.

OUTLETS

BALLY OUTLET STORE
1 Bally Place
New Rochelle, NY 10801
914-576-3230

20 Enterprise Ave.
Secaucus, NJ 07094
201-864-3444
7 days

Joan & Gerry's Best Buy

Discounted up to 60% off retail, you'll find the same shoes, handbags, briefcases, leather and suede jackets, belts you've seen in their shops; mostly closeouts and discontinued merchandise, but the real thing nonetheless.

COACH BAG OUTLET
Main St.
Amagansett, NY 11930
516-267-3340
7 days
(shorter hours after Labor Day)

Joan & Gerry's Best Buy

If you know how much the real things cost, you'll understand why crowds flock here for irregular and discontinued items at 30-50% off retail.

DAN RIVER OUTLET
1001 W. Main St.
Danville, VA 24541
804-799-7256
Mon.-Sat.

Joan & Gerry's Best Buy

A terrific secret source for Dan River and Yves St. Laurent bedding supplies; slightly irregular and closeout stock, but it's hard to tell. It helps to know what you want before you tackle the huge selection.

ETIENNE AIGNER
47 Brunswick Ave.
Edison, N.J.
908-248-1945
7 days

You've seen their classy shoes, handbags, blouses, and leather coats at the best department stores; here, you'll find them at 30% off retail prices.

THE FACTORY OUTLETS AT NORWALK
East Ave.
Norwalk, CT 06855
203-838-1349
7 days

Joan & Gerry's Best Buy

Great for housewares, this 26-store mall includes Bed Bath & Beyond, Company Store, Royal Doulton, and Old Mill; men's, women's, and kidswear outlets, too.

HARMON COVE OUTLET CENTER
20 Enterprise Ave.
Secaucus, NJ 07096
201-348-4780
7 days

Joan & Gerry's Best Buy

To New Yorkers, Secaucus means bargains; this place proves it, with 50 high-end stores from American Tourister luggage to Bally shoes.

LIBERTY VILLAGE OUTLETS
1 Church St.
Flemington NJ 08822
908-782-8550
7 days
(Call for extended holiday hours)

Joan & Gerry's Best Buy

Who says you have to trek to Maine for great outlet shopping? Just outside the city, you'll find names like Anne Klein, Joan and David, Calvin Klein, Corning/Revere, Villeroy & Boch, Jones New York, and Bass here.

LIZ CLAIBORNE
2 Emerson Lane
Secaucus, NJ 07096
201-319-8411
7 days

Joan & Gerry's Best Buy

Marked-down versions of her ubiquitous women's and menswear.

OUTLETS AT THE COVE
45 Meadowlands Parkway
Secaucus, NJ 07096
201-866-3516
7 days

Joan & Gerry's Best Buy
Only ten stores, but upmarket and classy. Among them: Fenn Wright & Manson, Harve Benard II, Jones New York, Van Heusen.

THE OUTLET STORE
77 Metro Way
Secaucus, NJ 07094
201-601-8700
7 days

Joan & Gerry's Best Buy
They wouldn't name names, but you'll find conservative American-look suits, sportswear, ties, belts, and socks here at a discount.

RDM (RINA Di MONTELLA) FACTORY OUTLET
2nd and Fayette
Conshohocken, PA 19428
215-834-0367
Mon.-Sat.

Joan & Gerry's Best Buy
Middle-of-nowhere outlet boasts a fabulous selection of evening dresses in silks, laces, sequins, and beads, always half off retail from $99-$580.

READING OUTLET CENTER
801 North 9th St.
Reading, PA 19604
215-373-5495
Mon.-Sat.

Joan & Gerry's Best Buy
You'll need a full day and lots of stamina to explore the 75 stores here; everything from Bass Shoes to Dooney & Burke handbags to Kitchen Collection.

UNITED STATUS APPAREL
25 Enterprise Ave.
Secaucus, NJ 07094
201-867-4455
Sat.-Thurs.

Joan & Gerry's Best Buy
Behind the generic facade, there's real name-brand womenswear here from Evan-Picone, J.H. Collectibles, and Jones New York at deep discounts.

WALLACH'S OUTLET
31-00 47th Ave.
Long Island City, NY 11101
718-482-8442
Wed.-Sun.

Joan & Gerry's Best Buy
At least half off retail for impressive men's shirts, coats, suits, shoes from names like Tripler, Roots, Chaps; much more from overstocks of national

*men's store chains. You'll find limited wom-
enswear from their Barrie Pace collection.*

WOODBURY COMMON
FACTORY OUTLETS
Route 23
Tower Building
Central Valley, NY 10917
914-928-7467
7 days
(May-end of December Thurs., Fri. until 9)

Joan & Gerry's Best Buy

*With 95 outlets vying for attention, you have to
shop strategically here; names you'd never expect
to see, like Adidas, Carlos Falchi, Tahari, Carole
Little, Brooks Brothers, Donna Karan, Escada,
Jones New York.*

PHOTO EQUIPMENT
& SUPPLIES

B & H PHOTO & ELECTRONICS
119 W. 17th St.
212-807-7474
Sun.-Fri.

*All the photographers come here for deals on pro-
fessional equipment; amateur shutterbugs will
find great prices on cameras, lenses, and supplies.*

47TH ST. PHOTO
67 W. 47th St.
115 W. 45th St.
212-398-1410
800-221-7774 (outside of N.Y. state)
718-722-4750 (mail order)
Sun.-Fri.

*Lines here for electronics bargains can fill a sub-
way station, but once you reach the counter you'll
find the staff helpful and the selection vast. Still,
we've found many items cheaper downtown; compare first.*

KEN HANSEN PHOTOGRAPHIC
920 Broadway, 2nd floor
212-777-5900
Mon.-Fri.

*No discounts here, but you get ultraprofessional
salespeople who know cameras inside out; names
like Hasselblad, Rolleiflex, Nikon, Contax, along
with terrific selections of computers, lighting, and
electronic imaging equipment.*

OLDEN CAMERA
1265 Broadway
212-725-1234
7 days

*After 55 years, this family-owned business has
earned undying loyalty of many NYC camera
buffs; polyglot salespeople can also help you find
discounted cameras, video equipment, computers,
cellular phones, and faxes.*

PICTURES, POSTERS, & PRINTS

GALLERY OF GRAPHIC ARTS
1601 York Ave.
212-988-4731
Mon.-Sat.

From just $50 to much higher, you'll find a superb collection of graphic art from around the world here; they also specialize in unusual framing jobs.

POSTER AMERICA
138 W. 18th St.
212-206-0499
Tues.-Sun.

Museum-quality European posters and graphic design ephemera line the walls of this Chelsea must-see. Original advertising art from 1910-`65, stunning design-movement posters, postcards, brochures, and collectible magazines.

PLASTICS

PLASTIC PARADISE
325 Canal St.
212-925-6782
7 days
Joan & Gerry's Best Buy

For shelves or dividers, this place will cut plastic to any size you need; terrific prices on invaluable plastic storage boxes, too.

PLEXI-CRAFT
514 W. 24th St.
212-924-3244
Mon.-Sat.

Since they manufacture their own TV stands, telephone stands, cubes, and shelving, prices come in close to wholesale; custom work, too.

QUILTS & QUILTING

AMERICA HURRAH
766 Madison Ave.
212-535-1930
Tues.-Sat. (closed Sat. in summer)
no c.c.

If they haven't already, quilt collectors should make a beeline here, with bags of money in hand; they'll find extraordinary quilts in mint condition along with rugs, painted furniture, baskets, rugs, and more collectible Americana.

J. SCHACHTER
85 Ludlow St.
212-533-1150
Sun.-Fri.

Exceptional custom quilts, sofa cushions, sleep and throw pillows; they'll also restuff, mend, and sew to make sofa cushions look like new. Terrific discounts on bed and bath linens, too.

THOS. K WOODARD AMERICAN ANTIQUES AND QUILTS
799 Madison Ave.
212-794-9404, 212-988-2906
Mon.-Sat. (closed Sat. in July and Aug.)

Coveted quilts, carpets, and American antiques; Woodard and his wife are world-renowned experts.

QUILTER'S PASSION
531 Amsterdam Ave.
212-580-2621
7 days

For quilting fanatics, this is the only source in the City; along with fabrics, supplies, and books, they offer quiltmaking classes.

RECORDS, TAPES, & CD'S

BLEECKER BOB'S GOLDEN OLDIE RECORD SHOP
118 W. Third St.
212-475-9677
7 days

*Whatever your taste in contemporary music —
Pink Floyd to Psychedelic Furs, Beatles to
Bauhaus — you'll find it here, one of the few
Manhattan stores that still stocks vinyl along with
CDs. No classical.*

DAYTON'S RECORD ARCHIVE
799 Broadway, room 210
212-254-5084
Mon.-Sat.
No c.c.

*With records nearing extinction, this source has
become more valuable than ever; aside from an
enormous stock, they'll track down hard-to-find
discs.*

FOOTLIGHT RECORDS
113 E. 12th St.
212-533-1572
7 days

*From the `40s through the `60s, you'll find an
enormous collection of Broadway musical cast
albums, movie soundtracks, chanteuses, and
crooners here; if they don't stock it, they'll hunt it
down.*

THE JAZZ RECORD CENTER
236 W. 26th St.
212-675-4480
Tues.-Sat.

A secret source — and a true find — for jazz lovers; opinionated, omniscient staff can direct you through huge stock of jazz records and books.

SOUNDS

20 St. Marks Place	212-677-3444
16 St. Marks Place	212-677-2727
7 days	
no c.c.	

Joan & Gerry's Best Buy

As if the compact discs here weren't cheap enough — at least $2-$3 off retail — this place has huge bins of used CDs for even less. No classical, but if you're looking for rock, dance, or soundtracks, check here first.

SHOES

SHOES — Children's

LITTLE ERIC

1331 Third Ave.	212-288-8987
590 Columbus Ave.	212-769-1610
1118 Madison Ave.	212-717-1513

Mon.-Sat.; Columbus Ave. store open Sun.

If you don't mind spending big money on shoes the little ones will probably outgrow in six months, come here; you'll find a very impressive selection of Italian and designer styles.

SHOES — General

AMS SHOE
Industrial Park at 20 Aquarian Drive
Secaucus, NY
201-866-4835
7 days

Joan & Gerry's Best Buy
Generic-looking shoe outlet offers up to 25% off retail on big footwear names like Nunn Bush, Rockport, Dexter, Clark's, and Bostonian.

BERGDORF GOODMAN
754 Fifth Ave.
Mon.-Sat.

Hardly a secret source, but their women's shoe collection is one of the city's most stylish and best-priced; check the fifth floor for mid-price names, second floor for ultra-high-end.

BREATHLESS
23 W. 36th St., 4th floor
212-714-1800
Mon.-Sat.

Joan & Gerry's Best Buy
Labels here might leave you breathless, but prices won't; near-wholesale shoes from Anne Klein, Perry Ellis Portfolio, Stuart Weitzman, Rosina Ferragamo.

CARLYLE BOOTERY
143 W. 33rd St.
212-564-1490
Mon.-Sat.

Joan & Gerry's Best Buy

Few name brands here, but good-looking shoes for less than $100; extra-wide sizes, too. Worth the short walk if you're shopping Macy's.

DUNHAM
PO Box 813
Brattleboro, VT 05302
800-544-4202

Joan & Gerry's Best Buy

Buying footwear by mail is a crapshoot, but this catalog makes it worthwhile; solid, handsome boots, boat shoes, and walking shoes for less than retail.

FRANKEL'S BOOTS
3924 Third Ave.
Brooklyn, N.Y.
718-788-9402, 718-768-9788
Tues.-Sat.

Joan & Gerry's Best Buy

Big-city style without Manhattan price tags; Justin and Dan Post cowboy boots, Timberland and Doc Martens shoes, Ray-Ban and Vuarnet sunglasses.

HARRY'S SHOES
2299 Broadway
212-874-2035
Mon.-Sat.

Weekends, whole families seem to shop here; men's, women's, and kids Rockport, Dexter, Bally, New Balance at fair prices. Narrow and wide sizes, too.

J. SHERMAN SHOES
121 Division St.
212-233-7898
Sun.-Fri.

Joan & Gerry's Best Buy

Classy designer shoes from Switzerland, Italy, England, and the U.S. discounted from 20-70%; surprising names like Bruno Magli, Rockport, Timberland, Bostonian, and Clark in sizes 6-13..

LACE UP SHOE SHOP
110 Orchard St.
212-475-8040, or 800-488-LACE (5223)
Sun.-Fri.

Joan & Gerry's Best Buy

We've never seen names like this in a discount shop: High-class Arche, Joan & David Couture, Anne Klein for women, Mephisto for men. They're still not cheap, but much less than retail.

MEDICI
163 Fifth Ave.
212-260-4253
Sun.-Fri.

Joan & Gerry's Best Buy
Instead of faddish footwear you wear once and store forever, this place has classic, very stylish shoes, many for under $100.

NANA
138 Prince St.
212-274-0749
7 days

If your kids have been bugging you for Doc Martens shoes and you don't know from Dr. Scholl's, send them here; they'll find an enormous selection, including hard-to-find colors.

NEW YORK SHOE COMPANY
489 Third Ave.
212-685-4056
7 days

Your mouth will drop at the selection — Cole-Haan, Linea Aldo, Dardini, Versace, Van Eli, Mario Bruni for women and men — and fall further at the prices, usually 20% off retail.

99X
84 E. 10th St.
212-460-8599
7 days

Joan & Gerry's Best Buy
Outrageous shoes, many imported from England, for less than you think; one-of-a-kind styles — fortunately, in some cases — from local designers.

SOLE OF ITALY
125 Orchard St.
212-674-2662
Sun.-Fri.

Joan & Gerry's Best Buy

They won't let us name names, but they carry the same Italian shoes as the better department stores for much less.

STAPLETON SHOE COMPANY
68 Trinity Place
212-964-6329
Mon.-Fri.

Joan & Gerry's Best Buy

Anyone who wears size 15EEE is probably named Sasquatch, but this place has shoes for them anyway; discounted Bostonian, Bass-Weejun, Florsheim, Allen-Edmonds, and Rockport from size 5.

VOGEL BOOTS AND SHOES
19 Howard St.
212-925-2460
Mon.-Sat. (closed Sat. in summer)

Finding the Holy Grail is easier, but once you locate this shop you'll stay loyal for life; exceptional made-to-measure boots and shoes.

SHOES — Men's

FELLMAN LTD.
24 E. 44th St.   212-687-6788

102 Fulton St.   212-227-0012

Mon.-Sat.

Joan & Gerry's Best Buy

*Very respectable men's business shoes from Bally,
Bostonian, French Shriner discounted up to 35%
off retail; courteous service.*

J.M. WESTON
42 E. 57th St.
212-308-5655
Mon.-Sat.

*Exquisite custom-made men's shoes, crafted 80%
by hand, from $375-$1,600; if you can afford to
indulge, you'll feel like nobility in them.*

SHOES — Women's

ANBAR
93 Reade St.
212-964-4017
Mon.-Sat.; closed Sat. in summer

Joan & Gerry's Best Buy

*Name-brand ladies' shoes they wouldn't name, at
up to half-off regular retail; handbags, too.*

FRENCH SOLE
281 Columbus Ave.
212-875-8910

985 Lexington Ave.
212-737-2859
Mon.-Sat.

Joan & Gerry's Best Buy

*If you love Chanel flats but hate the price tags, the
ballet shoes from this place make a good, affordable substitute; unbelievable range of colors and
styles.*

PETER FOX
378 Amsterdam Ave
212-874-8899

105 Thompson St.
212-481-6359
7 days

*Whimsical, hyper-detailed women's shoes, boots,
and slippers; if Cyndi Lauper designed footwear
in the 17th century, it'd look like this.*

SHOES — *Shoe Repair*

EVELYN AND SAN
400 E. 83rd St.
212-628-7618
Mon.-Sat.
No c.c.

*Shoe saviors of the Upper East Side; even the
department stores bring damaged goods here.
Trust them for impeccable repair, dyeing, refinishing work.*

THE HOUSTON SHOE HOSPITAL
5215 Kirby Dr.
Houston, TX.
713-977-1150

Instead of buying new shoes, send the old ones to the hospital; they'll come back refreshed, rejuvenated, and looking like new. Around $36 for new sole and heels, plus shipping; same-day special orders for those shoe emergencies.

SHOES — Special Sizes

GIORDANO'S
1150 Second Ave.
212-688-7195
Mon.-Sat.

A blessing for petite feet: stylish shoes in small sizes only. Names like Via Spiga, Anne Klein, Liz Claiborne, Allure, and Evan-Picone in 4 medium to 6 1/2 narrow. Ask for their $3.00 catalog.

IN STEP
1230 Second Ave.
212-734-7484
Mon.-Sat.

Sophisticated styles for small-size feet from names like Stuart Weitzman, Bally, D'Rossana, Amalfi; sizes 3 1/2-6 1/2 medium and 5 1/2-6 1/2 narrow.

9 1/2 SHOES PLUS
115 E. 57th St.
212-758-9637
Mon.-Sat

*Big feet don't have to mean clunky shoes; here, in
sizes 9 1/2-12, you'll find stylish Stuart
Weitzman, Pancaldi, Cole-Haan, and Via Spiga
from $100.*

SILVER

EASTERN SILVER COMPANY
54 Canal St., 2nd fl.
212-226-5708
Sun.-Thurs.

*Top-secret source for beautiful silver and pewter at
bargain prices, including many Jewish ceremoni-
al items.*

PATTERN FINDERS
P.O. Box 206
Port Jefferson Station, NY 11776
516-928-5158
Mail Order only

*If you thought you couldn't replace that missing
fork from Grandma's heirloom silver, call these
people; if they don't stock the elusive piece, they'll
trace it for a fee.*

SPECIALTY SHOPS

ALTAR EGOS
110 W. Houston St.
212-677-9588
7 days

Shopping here is a religious experience; they have paraphernalia from every faith on Earth, from elaborate crosses to images of Eastern divinities.

ASIAN HOUSE
888 Seventh Ave.
212-581-2294
Mon.-Sat.

Spectacular Oriental objets d'art *from China, Japan, Korea, Thailand, India, and the Philippines; you might think prices are in yen.*

CRAFT CARAVAN
63 Greene St.
212-431-6669
7 days

In a capacious Soho space that feels as big as the continent itself, you'll find an incredible choice of African jewelry, clothes, toys, accessories, and knick-knacks.

DRAGON GATE IMPORT AND EXPORT CO.
1115 Broadway
212-691-8600
Mon.-Sat.

Mostly from China, this place imports hand-carved Asian arts; you'll find antiques, jade, ivory, and stone carvings, bronze figurines.

HAMMOCK WORLD
66 E. 7th St.
212-673-1910
Mon.-Sat.

Travel south of the border without leaving the East Village; the authentic Mexican pottery, clothing, and toys here will transport you.

HOUSE OF NUBIAN
1 W. 8th St.
212-475-7553
7 days

East Village newcomer boasts impressive selection of authentic African items, as well as Black American memorabilia.

KOTO
71 W. Houston St.
212-533-8610
7 days

Brave souls who attempt to make their own sushi can find dishes and supplies here, along with authentic Japanese dining accessories.

MAGICKAL CHILDE
35 W. 19th St.
212-242-7182
7 days

*Bubble, bubble? Toil and trouble? Forget it.
Witchcraft these days means crystals, candles,
and talismans, and you'll find them here.*

OLD JAPAN
382 Bleecker St.
212-633-0922
Wed.-Mon.

*Beautiful Japanese kettles, jewelry boxes, and
porcelain; kimonos, too, from $20 (for cotton) to
$250 (for antique silk).*

ONLY HEARTS
386 Columbus Ave.
212-724-5608
7 days

*Diehard romantics should check out the heart-
shaped or -printed jewelry, balloons, pillows,
soaps, and even heart-topped plungers here;
unusual lingerie, too.*

RUSSIAN ARTS
451 Sixth Ave.
212-242-5946
Tues.-Sun.

*Fascinating little store-cum-museum filled with
Soviet memorabilia like military uniforms, pins,
and medals; the Russian dolls and decorative
items are wonderful.*

VISION OF TIBET
167 Thompson St.
212-995-9276
7 days

Direct from the land of the Dalai Lama, this place has beautiful hand-woven fabrics, clothes, jewelry, accessories; books, too.

SPORTING GOODS

CAPITOL FISHING
TACKLE COMPANY
218 W. 23rd St.
212-929-6132
Mon.-Sat.

The moon seems a more likely place than Manhattan for a fishing store, but this century-old business keeps thriving; unbeatable bargains on tackle and equipment from names like Penn, Shimano, Tycoon, Finnor, Garcia, and Daiwa keep serious anglers hooked.

G & S SPORTING GOODS
43 Essex St.
212-777-7950

Better-than-average prices on first-rate athletic footwear from big names like Nike, Reebok, New Balance, Keds; balls, gloves, and sports clothing, too.

GERRY COSBY AND COMPANY
3 Pennsylvania Plaza (Madison Square Garden)
212-563-6464
7 days
(open until game time before every Ranger and Knick game in the Garden)

Enormous selection of pro sports jerseys, NFL and NBA licensed apparel, pins, stickers, cups, and pennants; great for baseball caps, still the year's best accessory.

GOLDBERG'S MARINE
12 W. 37th St.
212-594-6065
7 days

Most people on this garment center block fish for clothing bargains, but you can find equipment for real fishing here; complete range of tackle, equipment, and nautical acessories.

H. KAUFFMAN AND SONS
419 Park Ave. South
212-684-6060
800-US-BOOTS(outside NY state)
7 days

You've seen gorgeous riding clothes in the fashion magazines; here's where the horsey set gets theirs. Jodphurs, shirts, hats for wannabes, saddles and bridles for real riders.

HICKORY AND TWEED
410 Main St.
Armonk, NY 10504
914-273-3397
Mon.-Sat.

A terrific "family leasing program" makes a trip to this ski-and-sports shop worthwhile; you buy the bindings, they'll outfit you and yours in top-quality equipment.

McCREEDY AND SCHREIBER
213 E. 59th St.   212-759-9241

37 W. 46th St.   212-719-1552
7 days

Camping department store with a mammoth selection of Frye, Justin, Larry Mahan, Timberland, Lucchese boots, some up to size 15.

MASON'S TENNIS MART
911 Seventh Ave.
212-757-5374
Mon.-Sat.

Everything for tennis enthusiasts except the court; their exceptional service includes same-day racket restringing.

NEW YORK GOLF CENTER
131 W. 35th St.
212-564-2255
Mon.-Sat.

Before they tee off, golf pros and amateurs alike cart away their clubs, bags, and equipment from here; the biggest selection from names like Callaway, Titleist, Wilson, Maruman, Honma, around 20% less than retail.

PARAGON SPORTING GOODS
867 Broadway
212-255-8036
7 days

Sporting goods department store carries everything from skis, skateboards, and sneakers to golf, hiking, camping, and sailing essentials over 80,000 square feet.

PECK & GOODIE
919 Eighth Ave.
212-246-6123
7 days

Ice skating stars come here to buy and sharpen skates; for your own ice capades, you'll find the City's best selection of novice-to-expert skates.

SPIEGEL'S
105 Nassau St.
212-227-8400
Mon.-Sat.

Complete equipment needs for any sport, as well as team orders; check out the selection of discounted CB winter jackets.

THE SPOT
19 E. 7th St
212-477-7590
7 days

New York's Skateboard Central; one of the City's best selections of boards and accessories.

STATIONERY

KATE'S PAPERIE
561 Broadway
212-941-9816
7 days

Stationery store on steroids stocks thousands of kinds of wrapping papers, boxes, cards, holiday ornaments, frames, photo albums at better-than-retail prices.

MARCIA KAHAN
46 Rose Lane
East Rockaway, NY 11518
516-374-1167

Good source for gorgeous invitations at great prices; discount social stationary, too.

RITE STATIONERY
113 Ludlow St.
212-477-0280; 212-477-1724
Sun.-Fri.

Joan & Gerry's Best Buy

So it's not Tiffany's. But if you have to stock up on notebooks and school supplies for the kids, it's worth the trip down here.

UNTITLED
159 Prince St.
212-982-2088
7 days

If you can't own a real Matisse, Magritte, or Monet, at least you get beautiful reproduction art cards, and this place has thousands of them from all periods.

TRAVEL

TRAVEL — Services

TRAVEL BARGAINS
800/872-8385

Joan & Gerry's Best Buy

For travel bargains, it's rumored that this number connects you with a major airline's very own "bucket shop"; this Philadelphia-based company also offers unbeatable deals on other international and domestic carriers.

800/FLY-CHEAP
800/CRUISE-CHEAP

Joan & Gerry's Best Buy

In case you can't tell from the phone numbers, they specialize in discount airfares and cruise deals; deep discounts on dozens of domestic flights. Of course, restrictions and advance-purchase rules apply.

ENCORE TRAVEL CLUB
800/638-8976

Joan & Gerry's Best Buy

Up to 50% off rack rates at major hotel chains here and in Europe; first-class travelers should ask about the unbelievable "Villas of the World" program for bargains at Europe's top properties.

UNITRAVEL
800/325-2222

Joan & Gerry's Best Buy

St. Louis-based consolidator sells seats the airlines can't unload themselves; for you, that means cheap tickets to Europe, the Far East, Australia, Africa, and South & Central America — you name it.

WHITE TRAVEL
800/547-4790

Joan & Gerry's Best Buy

From West Hartford, CT, this company cuts cruise deals that slice 5-65% off the cost of setting sail in style; volume gives them clout with the cruise companies.

TRAVEL — Supplies

THE CIVILIZED TRAVELLER
1072 Third Ave.
212-758-8305

World Financial Center
Vesey & West Sts.
Winter Garden, ground floor level
212-786-3301
7 days

Instead of frantically searching for last-minute necessities, frequent flyers, sailors, and hikers should visit this under-one-roof lifesaver; everything from packable rainwear to pocket tailors to portable showers.

UMBRELLAS

UNCLE SAM UMBRELLA SHOP
161 W. 57th St.
212-582-1976
Mon.-Sat.

This is the place where chic Upper East Siders buy umbrellas; if you're into status raingear, and money's no object, take a look.

WATCHES

ALAN MARCUS AND COMPANY
815 Connecticut Ave. NW, Suite 204
Washington, D.C. 20006
202-331-0671
Phones open Mon.-Fri.
No c.c.

Joan & Gerry's Best Buy

Find your dream watch, then call Marcus with the model number. You'll get discounts on Swiss timepieces from 22 brands, including Rolex, Cartier, Breguet, and Tagheuer. Jewelry and crystal too; call for catalog.

GEORGE PAUL JEWELERS
51 E. 58th St.
212-838-7660
Mon.-Fri.; Sat. in winter

Band-aid: This place carries one of the widest selections of watchbands we've ever seen, from leather to gold to buffalo and frog.

WIGS

RUTH WEINTRAUB COMPANY
420 Madison Ave.
212-838-1333
Mon.-Fri.; second Sat. of each month
By appointment only

Weintraub's creations are to wigs what couture is to clothing; starting at $2,000, each wig takes three sittings over about three weeks.

THERESA'S WIGS
217 E. 60th St.
212-486-1693
Mon.-Sat.

Terrific selection of custom wigs and hairpieces; the place to go for expert hairweaving, too.

DEPARTMENT-STORE SHOPPING SERVICES

These services are some of New York's best-kept shopping secrets. If you have no time, patience, or energy to jockey through crowded aisles and cluttered racks, department store shoppers can do the work for you. Most of them will even pick and send gifts — a chore we often wish we could leave to others. Best of all, you don't have to be a big spender to take advantage; all of these services are open to anyone, with no minimum purchase. They only ask that you call for an appointment.

BLOOMINGDALE'S

AT YOUR SERVICE: Sylvia Spitalnick, 212-705-3135.

These people are experts at putting wardrobes together for busy people, and they really get to know your what you like and what your lifestyle demands; they'll choose items and deliver, too.

HOPE'S CORNER: Hope Golden, 212-705-3375

If you can't spend hours browsing, call her for help navigating Bloomie's huge variety; she makes the shopping experience simpler and quicker.

AT HIS SERVICE: Frank Levandoski, 212-705-3030

From suits to socks, they'll help ultrabusy men select a wardrobe and deliver to home or office.

BEATRICE DALE CORPORATE SERVICES: Dale Shumate, 212-705-2378

This do-everything corporate gift service saves execs both time and headaches. If late hours at the office keep you from shopping, call them; they can arrange a visit before or after regular hours when the peons shop. New: Services especially for Japanese shoppers.

SHOP FOR WOMEN: Sandi Alpert, 212-705-2363

The ladies here are professionals who know how to put together a flattering wardrobe in larger sizes.

SHOP FOR PETITES: Jane Klein, 212-705-3005

Along with great ideas, Klein can keep you up on the latest news in petite fashions.

BRIDAL REGISTRY: Carol Spellman, 212-705-2800

You already know they do weddings, but they'll also help organize a storewide gift list for any occasion and simultaneously register the recipient at Bloomies nationwide.

INTERIOR DESIGN: Richard Knapple/Eileen Joyce, 212-705-2590

For a single piece of furniture or a total redecoration, they offer good advice — and taste.

MACY'S
BY APPOINTMENT
Linda Lee and staff

212-560-4181

Shopping doesn't get more personal than this: Call, tell them what you want in what price point, and they'll have it waiting for you in your own private fitting room.

LORD & TAYLOR
RED ROSE SHOPPING SERVICE
212-391-3344

A personal shopper will accompany you around the store to help you make decisions, or actually select merchandise for you.

BERGDORF GOODMAN
PERSONAL SHOPPING
212-753-7300

You always work with the same shopper here, so they really get to know you; good thing, since you can't take chances on such high-ticket goods. They'll mail out gifts, too.

PERSONAL SHOPPERS

If you hate waiting for sample sales, and you want the good stuff, a personal shopper can get it for you wholesale all year round. Most charge commissions from 15-20%, but you'll still come out way ahead of retail for designer and couture clothing.

Personal shoppers also let you see a much wider selection than the department stores. Stores have cut back orders in this economy, and the racks reflect it. Since these shoppers take you to the showrooms and contractors, you get to choose from almost everything, not just what a buyer thought would sell.

Before we name names, a disclaimer: Big mouths don't survive in this business, so we're not going to hint which designers these fashion mavens can get. But if you become a client, their secrets become yours.

MR. EDWARD: 212-874-7081
Not a shopper, he says, but "a fashion consultant who works with the showrooms." Specializes in

unusual sources; one lady he works with from London flies in with trunkloads of discount cashmere. He also gets to some European designers who hardly ever sell wholesale. Commission: 15%.

MARGOT GREEN: 212-772-0892

Green specializes in unique knits and silks, as well as "adaptations" of the top European and American couturiers. From January 1 through March, she works from Palm Beach. Won't specify commission.

GAIL KITTENPLAN ASSOCIATES: 212-348-8401

One of the few who shops for men as well as women, Kittenplan also does corporate and bridal gifts; special-occasion clothing makes up the bulk of her business. Commission: 20%.

MARJORIE STOKES: 212-PL3-0033

Doyenne *of personal shoppers. Ultra-discreet and charming, she only does "upper-end" American designers up to half off retail for an "elite" clientele from all over the world. Not surprisingly, she won't specify her commission.*